Nancy Wentworth, PhD
Rodney Earle, PhD
Michael L. Connell, PhD
Editors

Integrating Information Technology into the Teacher Education Curriculum: Process and Products of Change

Integrating Information Technology into the Teacher Education Curriculum: Process and Products of Change has been co-published simultaneously as *Computers in the Schools*, Volume 21, Numbers 1/2 2004.

Pre-publication REVIEWS, COMMENTARIES, EVALUATIONS . . .

"If you are looking for A VALUABLE 'HOW-TO' VOLUME on technology integration from various areas across the educational landscape, this text is one that OFFERS AN ABUNDANCE OF IDEAS AND RESEARCH. This collection provides a superb example, showing how Brigham Young University made important, far-reaching changes by integrating technology into the learning process for both faculty and students in the School of Education."

Mitchell O. Pratt, PhD
Adjunct Professor
Instructional Psychology and Technology Department, David O. McKay School of Education, Brigham Young University

The Haworth Press, Inc.

Integrating Information Technology into the Teacher Education Curriculum: Process and Products of Change

Integrating Information Technology into the Teacher Education Curriculum: Process and Products of Change has been co-published simultaneously as *Computers in the Schools*, Volume 21, Numbers 1/2 2004.

The *Computers in the Schools* Monographic "Separates"

Below is a list of "separates," which in serials librarianship means a special issue simultaneously published as a special journal issue or double-issue *and* as a "separate" hardbound monograph. (This is a format which we also call a "DocuSerial.")

"Separates" are published because specialized libraries or professionals may wish to purchase a specific thematic issue by itself in a format which can be separately cataloged and shelved, as opposed to purchasing the journal on an on-going basis. Faculty members may also more easily consider a "separate" for classroom adoption.

"Separates" are carefully classified separately with the major book jobbers so that the journal tie-in can be noted on new book order slips to avoid duplicate purchasing.

You may wish to visit Haworth's website at . . .

http://www.HaworthPress.com

. . . to search our online catalog for complete tables of contents of these separates and related publications.

You may also call 1-800-HAWORTH (outside US/Canada: 607-722-5857), or Fax 1-800-895-0582 (outside US/Canada: 607-771-0012), or e-mail at:

docdelivery@haworthpress.com

Integrating Information Technology into the Teacher Education Curriculum: Process and Products of Change, edited by Nancy Wentworth, PhD, Rodney Earle, PhD, and Michael L. Connell, PhD (Vol. 21, No. 1/2, 2004). *A powerful reference for teacher education departments striving to integrate new technologies into their curriculum and motivate their faculty to utilize them.*

Distance Education: What Works Well, edited by Michael Corry, PhD, and Chih-Hsuing Tu, PhD (Vol. 20, No. 3, 2003). *"A must read. . . . Provides a highly readable, practical, yet critical perspective into the design, delivery, and implementation of distance learning. . . . Examines issues faced by distance educators, offers valuable tactics culled from experience, and outlines strategies that have been key success factors for a wide variety of distance learning initiatives." (Veena Mahesh, PhD, Distance and Blended Learning Program Manager, Technology Manufacturing Group Training, Intel Corporation)*

Technology in Education: A Twenty-Year Retrospective, edited by D. LaMont Johnson, PhD, and Cleborne D. Maddux, PhD (Vol. 20, No. 1/2, 2003). *"Interesting, informative, relevant. . . . Having so many experts between the covers of one book was a treat. . . . I enjoyed reading this book!" (Susan W. Brown, PhD, Science/Math Methods Professor and Professional Curriculum Coordinator, New Mexico State University)*

Distance Education: Issues and Concerns, edited by Cleborne D. Maddux, PhD, Jacque Ewing-Taylor, MS, and D. LaMont Johnson, PhD (Vol. 19, No. 3/4, 2002). *Provides practical, research-based advice on distance education course design.*

Evaluation and Assessment in Educational Information Technology, edited by Leping Liu, PhD, D. LaMont Johnson, PhD, Cleborne D. Maddux, PhD, and Norma J. Henderson, MS (Vol. 18, No. 2/3 and 4, 2001). *Explores current trends, issues, strategies, and methods of evaluation and assessment in educational information technology.*

The Web in Higher Education: Assessing the Impact and Fulfilling the Potential, edited by Cleborne D. Maddux, PhD, and D. LaMont Johnson, PhD (Vol. 17, No. 3/4 and Vol. 18, No. 1, 2001). *"I enthusiastically recommend this book to anyone new to Web-based program development. I am certain that my project has moved along more rapidly because of what I learned from this text. The chapter on designing online education courses helped to organize my programmatic thinking. Another chapter did an outstanding job of debunking the myths regarding Web learning." (Carol Swift, PhD, Associate Professor and Chair of the Department of Human Development and Child Studies, Oakland University, Rochester, Michigan)*

Using Information Technology in Mathematics Education, edited by D. James Tooke, PhD, and Norma Henderson, MS (Vol. 17, No. 1/2, 2001). *"Provides thought-provoking material on several aspects and levels of mathematics education. The ideas presented will provide food for thought for the reader, suggest new methods for the classroom, and give new ideas for further research." (Charles E. Lamb, EdD, Professor, Mathematics Education, Department of Teaching, Learning, and Culture, College of Education, Texas A&M University, College Station)*

Integration of Technology into the Classroom: Case Studies, edited by D. LaMont Johnson, PhD, Cleborne D. Maddux, PhD, and Leping Liu, PhD (Vol. 16, No. 2/3/4, 2000). *Use these fascinating case studies to understand why bringing information technology into your classroom can make you a more effective teacher, and how to go about it!*

Information Technology in Educational Research and Statistics, edited by Leping Liu, PhD, D. LaMont Johnson, PhD, and Cleborne D. Maddux, PhD (Vol. 15, No. 3/4, and Vol. 16, No. 1, 1999). *This important book focuses on creating new ideas for using educational technologies such as the Internet, the World Wide Web and various software packages to further research and statistics. You will explore on-going debates relating to the theory of research, research methodology, and successful practices.* Information Technology in Educational Research and Statistics *also covers the debate on what statistical procedures are appropriate for what kinds of research designs.*

Educational Computing in the Schools: Technology, Communication, and Literacy, edited by Jay Blanchard, PhD (Vol. 15, No. 1, 1999). *Examines critical issues of technology, teaching, and learning in three areas: access, communication, and literacy. You will discover new ideas and practices for gaining access to and using technology in education from preschool through higher education.*

Logo: A Retrospective, edited by Cleborne D. Maddux, PhD, and D. LaMont Johnson, PhD (Vol. 14, No. 1/2, 1997). *"This book–honest and optimistic–is a must for those interested in any aspect of Logo: its history, the effects of its use, or its general role in education." (Dorothy M. Fitch, Logo consultant, writer, and editor, Derry, New Hampshire)*

Using Technology in the Classroom, edited by D. LaMont Johnson, PhD, Cleborne D. Maddux, PhD, and Leping Liu, MS (Vol. 13, No. 1/2, 1997). *"A guide to teaching with technology that emphasizes the advantages of transiting from teacher-directed learning to learner-centered learning–a shift that can draw in even 'at-risk' kids." (Book News, Inc.)*

Multimedia and Megachange: New Roles for Educational Computing, edited by W. Michael Reed, PhD, John K. Burton, PhD, and Min Liu, EdD (Vol. 10, No. 1/2/3/4, 1995). *"Describes and analyzes issues and trends that might set research and development agenda for educators in the near future." (Sci Tech Book News)*

Language Minority Students and Computers, edited by Christian J. Faltis, PhD, and Robert A. DeVillar, PhD (Vol. 7, No. 1/2, 1990). *"Professionals in the field of language minority education, including ESL and bilingual education, will cheer this collection of articles written by highly respected, research-writers, along with computer technologists, and classroom practitioners." (Journal of Computing in Teacher Education)*

Logo: Methods and Curriculum for Teachers, by Cleborne D. Maddux, PhD, and D. LaMont Johnson, PhD (Supp #3, 1989). *"An excellent introduction to this programming language for children." (Rena B. Lewis, Professor, College of Education, San Diego State University)*

Assessing the Impact of Computer-Based Instruction: A Review of Recent Research, by M. D. Roblyer, PhD, W. H. Castine, PhD, and F. J. King, PhD (Vol. 5, No. 3/4, 1988). *"A comprehensive and up-to-date review of the effects of computer applications on student achievement and attitudes." (Measurements & Control)*

Educational Computing and Problem Solving, edited by W. Michael Reed, PhD, and John K. Burton, PhD (Vol. 4, No. 3/4, 1988). *Here is everything that educators will need to know to use computers to improve higher level skills such as problem solving and critical thinking.*

The Computer in Reading and Language Arts, edited by Jay S. Blanchard, PhD, and George E. Mason, PhD (Vol. 4, No. 1, 1987). *"All of the [chapters] in this collection are useful, guiding the teacher unfamiliar with classroom computer use through a large number of available software options and classroom strategies." (Educational Technology)*

Computers in the Special Education Classroom, edited by D. LaMont Johnson, PhD, Cleborne D. Maddux, PhD, and Ann Candler, PhD (Vol. 3, No. 3/4, 1987). *"A good introduction to the use of computers in special education. . . . Excellent for those who need to become familiar with computer usage with special population students because they are contemplating it or because they have actually just begun to do it." (Science Books and Films)*

You Can Do It/Together, by Kathleen A. Smith, PhD, Cleborne D. Maddux, PhD, and D. LaMont Johnson, PhD (Supp #2, 1986). *A self-instructional textbook with an emphasis on the partnership system of learning that introduces the reader to four critical areas of computer technology.*

Computers and Teacher Training: A Practical Guide, by Dennis M. Adams, PhD (Supp #1, 1986). *"A very fine . . . introduction to computer applications in education." (International Reading Association)*

The Computer as an Educational Tool, edited by Henry F. Olds, Jr. (Vol. 3, No. 1, 1986). *"The category of tool uses for computers holds the greatest promise for learning, and this . . . book, compiled from the experiences of a good mix of practitioners and theorists, explains how and why." (Jack Turner, Technology Coordinator, Eugene School District 4-J, Oregon)*

Logo in the Schools, edited by Cleborne D. Maddux, PhD (Vol. 2, No. 2/3, 1985). *"An excellent blend of enthusiasm for the language of Logo mixed with empirical analysis of the language's effectiveness as a means of promoting educational goals. A much-needed book!" (Rena Lewis, PhD, Professor, College of Education, San Diego State University)*

Humanistic Perspectives on Computers in the Schools, edited by Steven Harlow, PhD (Vol. 1, No. 4, 1985). *"A wide spectrum of information." (Infochange)*

Integrating Information Technology into the Teacher Education Curriculum: Process and Products of Change

Nancy Wentworth, PhD
Rodney Earle, PhD
Michael L. Connell, PhD
Editors

Integrating Information Technology into the Teacher Education Curriculum: Process and Products of Change has been co-published simultaneously as *Computers in the Schools*, Volume 21, Numbers 1/2 2004.

The Haworth Press, Inc.

New York • London • Victoria (AU)
www.HaworthPress.com

Integrating Information Technology into the Teacher Education Curriculum: Process and Products of Change has been co-published simultaneously as *Computers in the Schools*, Volume 21, Numbers 1/2 2004.

The development, preparation, and publication of this work has been undertaken with great care. However, the publisher, employees, editors, and agents of The Haworth Press and all imprints of The Haworth Press, Inc., including The Haworth Medical Press® and Pharmaceutical Products Press®, are not responsible for any errors contained herein or for consequences that may ensue from use of materials or information contained in this work. Opinions expressed by the author(s) are not necessarily those of The Haworth Press, Inc. With regard to case studies, identities and circumstances of individuals discussed herein have been changed to protect confidentiality. Any resemblance to actual persons, living or dead, is entirely coincidental.

Cover design by Kerry E. Mack

Library of Congress Cataloging-in-Publication Data

Integrating information technology into the teacher education curriculum : process and products of change / Nancy Wentworth, Rodney Earle, Michael L. Connell, editors.
     p. cm.
     "Integrating information technology into the teacher education curriculum : process and products of change has been co-published simultaneously as Computers in the schools, volume 21, numbers 1/2 2004."
     Includes bibliographical references and index.
     ISBN 0-7890-2627-9 (hard cover : alk. paper) – ISBN 0-7890-2628-7 (soft cover : alk. paper)
     1. Teachers–Training of–Curricula–Utah–Provo–Case studies. 2. Computer-assisted instruction–Utah–Provo–Case studies. 3. Information technology–Utah–Provo–Case studies. 4. David O. McKay School of Education–Case studies. I. Wentworth, Nancy. II. Earle, Rodney. III. Connell, Michael L., 1956- IV. Computers in the schools.
  LB1716.I58 2004
  370′.71′1–dc22
                                            2004014441

Indexing, Abstracting & Website/Internet Coverage

This section provides you with a list of major indexing & abstracting services. That is to say, each service began covering this periodical during the year noted in the right column. Most Websites which are listed below have indicated that they will either post, disseminate, compile, archive, cite or alert their own Website users with research-based content from this work. (This list is as current as the copyright date of this publication.)

Abstracting, Website/Indexing Coverage . . . . Year When Coverage Began

- *Abstracts in Social Gerontology: Current Literature on Aging* 2003
- *Academic Abstracts/CD-ROM* 1994
- *AURSI African Urban & Regional Science Index. A scholarly & research index which synthesises & compiles all publications on urbanization & regional science in Africa within the world. Published annually* 2004
- *Australian Education Index <http://www.acer.edu.au>* 2001
- *Business Source Corporate: coverage of nearly 3,350 quality magazines and journals; designed to meet the diverse information needs of corporations; EBSCO Publishing <http://www.epnet.com/corporate/bsourcecorp.asp>* 1994
- *Child Development Abstracts & Bibliography (in print & online) <http://www.ukans.edu>* 2000
- *Computer and Information Systems Abstracts <http://www.csa.com>* . . 2004
- *Computer Literature Index <http://www.clisearch.com>* 1993
- *Computing Reviews <http://www.reviews.com>* 1992
- *Criminal Justice Abstracts* . . . . *
- *Current Index to Journals in Education* 1991

(continued)

- *Education Abstracts. Published by The HW Wilson Company <http://www.hwwilson.com>* 1992
- *Education Digest* 1991
- *Education Index. Published by the HW Wilson Company (also available in electronic format) <http://www.hwwilson.com>* 1999
- *Education Process Improvement Ctr, Inc. (EPICENTER) <http://www.epicent.com>* 2000
- *Educational Administration Abstracts (EAA)* 1991
- *Educational Technology Abstracts* 1991
- *Engineering Information (PAGE ONE)* 1994
- *e-psyche, LLC <http://www.e-psyche.net>* 2003
- *Family Index Database <http://www.familyscholar.com>* 2004
- *IBZ International Bibliography of Periodical Literature <http://www.saur.de>* 1996
- *Index Guide to College Journals (core list compiled by integrating 48 indexes frequently used to support undergraduate programs in small to medium sized libraries)* 1999
- *Information Science & Technology Abstracts: indexes journal articles from more than 450 publications as well as books, research reports, conference proceedings; EBSCO Publishing <http://www.epnet.com>* 1994
- *INSPEC is the leading English-language bibliographic service providing access to the world's scientific & technical literature in physics, electrical engineering, electronics, communications, control engineering, computers & computing, and information technology <http://www.iee.org.uk/publish/>* 1984
- *International Bulletin of Bibliography on Education* 1991
- *Internationale Bibliographie der geistes- und sozialwissenschaftlichen Zeitschriftenliteratur . . . See IBZ* 1996
- *Internet & Personal Computing Abstracts (IPCA) (formerly Microcomputer Abstracts) provides access to concise and comprehensive information on the latest PC products & developments, covering over 120 of the most important publications; EBSCO Publishing <http://www.epnet.com/public/internet&personal.asp>* 2003
- *Linguistics & Language Behavior Abstracts (LLBA) <http://www.csa.com>* 1991
- *MasterFILE: Updated database from EBSCO Publishing* 1995

(continued)

- *MasterFILE Elite: Coverage of nearly 1,200 periodicals covering general reference, business, health, education, general science, multi-cultural issues and much more; EBSCO Publishing <http://www.epnet.com/government/mfelite.asp>* 1994
- *MasterFILE Premier: Coverage of more than 1,950 periodicals covering general reference, business, health, education, general science, multi-cultural issues and much more; EBSCO Publishing <http://www.epnet.com/government/mfpremier.asp>* 1994
- *MasterFILE Select: Coverage of nearly 770 periodicals covering general reference, business, health, education, general science, multi-cultural issues and much more; EBSCO Publishing <http://www.epnet.com/government/mfselect.asp>* 1994
- *Mathematical Didactics (MATHDI) <http://www.emis.de/MATH/DI.html>* 1995
- *MLA International Bibliography provides a classified listing & subject index for books & articles published on modern languages, literatures, folklore, & linguistics. Available in print and in several electronic versions. Indexes over 50,000 publications <http://www.mla.org>* . . . 2001
- *OCLC ArticleFirst <http://www.oclc.org/services/databases/>* 2001
- *OCLC ContentsFirst <http://www.oclc.org/services/databases/>* 2001
- *Professional Development Collection: Coverage of 530 professional development titles; EBSCO Publishing* 1994
- *ProQuest Education Complete. Contents of this publication are indexed and abstracted in the ProQuest Education Complete database (includes only abstracts . . . not full-text), available on ProQuest Information & Learning <http://www.proquest.com>* 1994
- *Referativnyi Zhurnal (Abstracts Journal of the All-Russian Institute of Scientific and Technical Information–in Russian)* . . . 1991
- *Social Work Abstracts <http://www.silverplatter.com/catalog/swab.htm>* 1991
- *Sociological Abstracts (SA) <http://www.csa.com>* 1991
- *Sociology of Education Abstracts* 1991
- *SwetsNet <http://www.swetsnet.com>* 2001
- *Wilson OmniFile Full Text: Mega Edition (only available electronically) <http://www.hwwilson.com>* 1992
- *ZDM/International Reviews on Mathematical Education <http://www.fiz-karlsruhe.de/fiz/publications/zdm/zdmp1/html>* . 1991

*Exact start date to come.

*Special Bibliographic Notes related to special journal issues
(separates) and indexing/abstracting:*

- indexing/abstracting services in this list will also cover material in any "separate" that is co-published simultaneously with Haworth's special thematic journal issue or DocuSerial. Indexing/abstracting usually covers material at the article/chapter level.
- monographic co-editions are intended for either non-subscribers or libraries which intend to purchase a second copy for their circulating collections.
- monographic co-editions are reported to all jobbers/wholesalers/approval plans. The source journal is listed as the "series" to assist the prevention of duplicate purchasing in the same manner utilized for books-in-series.
- to facilitate user/access services all indexing/abstracting services are encouraged to utilize the co-indexing entry note indicated at the bottom of the first page of each article/chapter/contribution.
- this is intended to assist a library user of any reference tool (whether print, electronic, online, or CD-ROM) to locate the monographic version if the library has purchased this version but not a subscription to the source journal.
- individual articles/chapters in any Haworth publication are also available through the Haworth Document Delivery Service (HDDS).

Integrating Information Technology into the Teacher Education Curriculum: Process and Products of Change

Contents

INTRODUCTION

Technology Integration into a Teacher Education Program
Nancy Wentworth
Gregory L. Waddoups
Rodney Earle　　1

Principles of Technology Integration and Curriculum Development:
A Faculty Design Team Approach
Gregory L. Waddoups
Nancy Wentworth
Rodney Earle　　15

Supporting Change in Teacher Education: Using Technology
as a Tool to Enhance Problem-Based Learning
Roni Jo Draper
Leigh Smith
Brenda Sabey　　25

The Power of Action Research, Technology
and Teacher Education
J. Merrell Hansen
Nancy Nalder-Godfrey　　43

Redesigning an Introduction to Special Education Course
by Infusing Technology
Tina Taylor Dyches
Barbara A. Smith
Suraj Syal　　59

Using Technology in Teacher Preparation: Two Mature Teacher
    Educators Negotiate the Steep Learning Curve

Eula Monroe

Marvin Tolman   73

Electronic Portfolios in Evolution

Roger Olsen   85

Developing Electronic Portfolios Across the State of Utah:
    Breaks, Breakdowns and Breakthroughs

Carol Lee Hawkins

Sharon Black   95

Faculty-as-Students: Teacher Education Faculty Meaningfully
    Engaged in a Pre-Service Technology Course

J. Aaron Popham

Rebecca Rocque   115

Redesigning the Teacher Education Technology Course
    to Emphasize Integration

Charles Graham

Richard Culatta

Mitchell Pratt

Richard West   127

Designing and Teaming on the Outside: Extending PT3 Efforts
    Across Campus, Across Five Districts and Across the State

Sharon Black   149

The View from Outside: 2000-2003

Michael L. Connell

D. LaMont Johnson   165

Index   185

ABOUT THE EDITORS

Nancy Wentworth, PhD, is Associate Professor of Teacher Education in the McKay School of Education at Brigham Young University, and serves on the board of the Utah Association of Teacher Education (UATE) and the Northern Rocky Mountain Educational Research Association (NRMERA). She was the principal investigator of the BYU Preparing Tomorrow's Teachers to Use Technology (PT3) federal grant. She works with secondary education candidates certifying in mathematics education. Her research interests include the integration of technology in K-12 and teacher education curriculum, constructivist learning, and partnerships with public education.

Rodney Earle, PhD, is Professor and Associate Chair of Teacher Education in the McKay School of Education at Brigham Young University, serves on the board of the Association for Educational Communications and Technology (AECT) and is AECT's liaison with the National Council for Accreditation of Teacher Education and senior editor of the AECT national technology standards. His thirty years of teaching include experiences at the elementary, secondary, and college levels in Australia, Canada, and the United States. His research interests focus on technology integration, instructional design, teacher planning processes, teacher imagery and metaphors, and phases of teaching.

Michael L. Connell, PhD, is Associate Professor of Curriculum and Instruction at the University of Houston, and is on the National Web Advisory Board of the National Council of Measurement in Education (NCME). He is the Director of the Center for Mathematics, Science, and Technology and member of the Academic Computing Advisory Committee at the University of Houston. He has served as the editor of the Mathematics Section of the Society of Information Technology and Teacher Education Annual for several years. He has published extensively on the use of technology cognitive representation of mathematics.

INTRODUCTION

Nancy Wentworth
Gregory L. Waddoups
Rodney Earle

Technology Integration into a Teacher Education Program

SUMMARY. The BYU PT3 grant focused on the integration of technology in our teacher education program and in the K-12 lessons developed by our students. This article describes the goals, objectives, and activities of our three-year BYU PT3 implementation grant and how they were implemented each year. We discuss the development of design teams made up of teacher education faculty, content-area faculty, and district curriculum and technology specialists. *[Article copies available for a fee from The Haworth Document Delivery Service: 1-800-HAWORTH. E-mail address: <docdelivery@haworthpress.com> Website: <http://www.HaworthPress.com> © 2004 by The Haworth Press, Inc. All rights reserved.]*

NANCY WENTWORTH is Associate Professor, Department of Teacher Education, Brigham Young University, Provo, UT 84602 (E-mail: nancy_wentworth@byu.edu).
GREGORY L. WADDOUPS is Director, Instructional Design and Evaluation, The Center for Instructional Design, Brigham Young University, Provo, UT 84602 (E-mail: greg_waddoups@byu.edu).
RODNEY EARLE is Professor and Associate Chair, Department of Teacher Education, Brigham Young University, Provo, UT 84602 (E-mail: rodney_earle@byu.edu).

[Haworth co-indexing entry note]: "Technology Integration into a Teacher Education Program." Wentworth, Nancy, Gregory L. Waddoups, and Rodney Earle. Co-published simultaneously in *Computers in the Schools* (The Haworth Press, Inc.) Vol. 21, No. 1/2, 2004, pp. 1-14; and: *Integrating Information Technology into the Teacher Education Curriculum: Process and Products of Change* (ed: Nancy Wentworth, Rodney Earle, and Michael L. Connell) The Haworth Press, Inc., 2004, pp. 1-14. Single or multiple copies of this article are available for a fee from The Haworth Document Delivery Service [1-800-HAWORTH, 9:00 a.m. - 5:00 p.m. (EST). E-mail address: docdelivery@haworthpress.com].

http://www.haworthpress.com/web/CITS
© 2004 by The Haworth Press, Inc. All rights reserved.
Digital Object Identifier: 10.1300/J025v21n01_01

1

KEYWORDS. Professional development, systemic change, technology integration

INTRODUCTION

Preparing tomorrow's teachers to use technology in schools is a complex endeavor requiring the infusion of technology into curriculum and instructional practices at all levels of the pre-service program. Too often both university instructors and public school teachers are unable or unwilling to integrate technology into their curricula (Strudler, Quinn, McKinney, & Jones, 1995; Willis, Willis, Austin, & Colón, 1995). There are a number of reasons for this: computer illiteracy, computer phobia, disinterest, lack of equipment, and lack of time to learn appropriate uses of technology in instruction. Technology instruction of university faculty, public school teachers, and pre-service teachers is often an introduction to computer software isolated from curriculum development (Wentworth, 1998). Most often the use of technology is not linked to methodology that supports real experiences for either pre-service teachers or public students.

THE PT3 PROGRAM

The federal grant program *Preparing Tomorrow's Teachers to Use Technology (PT3)* has supported the development of models for integrating technology into teacher education programs and K-12 curriculum. In many early teacher education programs prospective teachers took a computer literacy class separate from content methods classes and rarely engaged in real collaboration on how school teachers could integrate technology into authentic learning experiences (Kearsley, 1998). By focusing merely on how to use computers, technology training failed by not addressing how to teach students more effectively using a variety of technological tools. Kearsley further lamented the lack of technology preparation for teachers (too little and too late), stressing the realistic need for extensive and sustained practice over years, not one-day workshops (p. 49). What teachers need to know most is how to teach content more effectively. Because of the quick-fix mindset in education, programs "teach people how to use specific types of technology [rather than] how to solve educational problems using technology when needed and appropriate" (Kearsley, 1998, p. 50). Jostens' Learning

Corporation and the American Association of School Administrators reported that teacher training, while readily available, focuses merely on basic computer operation and fails to address helping teachers use technology to teach more effectively (Jostens, 1997). Many public school classrooms have not linked instruction to real-life situations or technology integration so the practical experiences of pre-service teachers have been limited (Pappillion & Cellitti, 1996). Technology integration should cause teachers to develop different perspectives through rethinking teaching and learning (Riedl, 1995; Ritchie & Wilburg, 1994). Teaching with technology causes teachers to confront their established beliefs about instruction and their traditional roles as classroom teachers.

The PT3-funded restructuring efforts of the BYU grant were designed to alleviate these weaknesses in traditional teacher preparation through simultaneous redesign of teacher preparation and K-12 curricula, enriching *both* with technology integration. Preparing tomorrow's teachers to integrate technology into their instruction requires university faculty to provide pre-service teachers with examples of and experiences with learning enhanced with technology. Teacher educators must adopt the knowledge, dispositions, and practices associated with effective technology integration. Successfully integrating technology into a teacher preparation program includes, at a minimum, rethinking curriculum and methods of instruction, providing mentoring and support for associated faculty members, and developing collaborative relationships among university faculty, pre-service teachers, teachers, and school districts.

The following articles will describe the teacher education program at Brigham Young University (BYU) and the implementation of our PT3 grant. The model developed implemented strategies for technology integration by creating curriculum design teams composed of university faculty, public school personnel, and instructional design and technology specialists.

BRIGHAM YOUNG UNIVERSITY MCKAY SCHOOL OF EDUCATION

The Brigham Young University McKay School of Education graduates over 1,000 teachers each year. These teacher education students enter the program in cohorts of approximately 30 and work together for two years in content, methods, and certification courses. While in cohorts, these students share both on-campus classroom time and public school experiences. Services are provided by a cohort team, which includes the university faculty supervisor, a Clinical Faculty Associate (CFA, an outstanding teacher from the public school who spends two years on campus), several university methods teachers, and public school personnel (mentor teachers and teacher leaders who are building-level facilitators). The BYU teacher education program currently provides lab access to modern technologies for students and requires pre-service teachers to take one instructional technology course. Prior to receiving the PT3 grant, there was support for faculty who self-selected to use technology in undergraduate courses, but there was not a systematic effort to integrate technology into the overall curriculum. Given the importance placed on technology integration by accreditation bodies, it was important to focus efforts and resources on moving more faculty to integrate technology into the curriculum.

Based on this history and the perceived need to move the faculty along in the effective use of technology, a concerted effort has been made to mentor faculty and build alignment around issues of technology integration. These goals have been achieved through three major project activities: (a) creating curriculum design teams composed of university faculty (including teacher education and content-specific methods instructors), and cooperating public school personnel; (b) holding yearly summer institutes and other training and collaboration opportunities that focus on the infusion of technology; and (c) facilitating alignment among McKay School activities, cooperating districts, the state office of education, and other teacher preparation programs in the state. In addition to these activities, informal lunchtime meetings provided venues for faculty to share their use of technology and allowed for just-in-time technical and instructional support to help the design teams as they learned to integrate technology.

The goals, objectives, and outcomes of the BYU PT3 grant centered around the NCATE standards and involved three groups of participants involved together with cohort teams: (a) BYU students participating as members of elementary, secondary, and special education cohorts; (b) BYU faculty including school of education faculty, CFAs, and arts and science faculty, particularly those teaching methods classes in core areas such as language arts, mathematics, science, and social studies; and (c) technology/curriculum specialists and cooperating teachers from partnership public schools. We planned activities that would involve all participants across the goals. The following is a summary of the BYU PT3 goals, objective, and outcomes:

Goal No. 1: BYU faculty will meet NCATE Standards related to faculty expertise with technology.

Objective a: BYU faculty members who work in the teacher education program will be "knowledgeable about current practice related to the use of computers and technology" (NCATE Standard).

- Activity: Cohort design teams consisting of technology/curriculum specialists from the public schools in the partnership districts, BYU faculty, and cooperating teachers from the school districts who incorporate technology successfully in their classrooms will review teacher preparation courses and K-12 curriculum.
- Activity: The design teams will assess the university faculty's ability to integrate technology.
- Activity: During monthly seminars design teams will mentor university faculty in the use of computers and technology (e.g., spreadsheets, presentation software, Internet access, scanners, digital cameras, Web site development).

Objective b: BYU faculty will "integrate technology into their teaching" (NCATE Standard).

- Activity: BYU faculty will implement at least three software applications into their teaching.
- Activity: BYU faculty will create online syllabi.
- Activity: BYU faculty will communicate with their students using e-mail and listserves.
- Activity: During monthly seminars the technology specialists will mentor university faculty as they integrate technology into their curriculum and create online syllabi and other curriculum material.

Objective c: BYU faculty will "apply tools for enhancing their own professional growth and productivity" (NCATE Standard) and in "communicating, collaboratively conducting research, and solving problems" (NCATE Standard).

- Activity: BYU faculty will research the effectiveness of technology integration in their teaching.
- Activity: BYU faculty who are on design teams will attend SITE and ISTE conferences to increase their understanding of technology in teacher education (travel funded by the grant).

- Activity: BYU faculty will report results of technology integration on the BYU technology Web site.
- Activity: Summer institutes will provide opportunities for the sharing of technology-rich curriculum.

Goal No. 2: BYU education and content area methods courses will meet the NCATE Standards for technology integration.

Objective a: BYU courses will require "students to develop an understanding of the structure, skills, core concepts, ideas, values, facts, methods of inquiry, and uses of technology for the subjects they plan to teach" (NCATE Standard).

- Activity: Design teams will examine Utah State K-12 Core Curricula for courses already rich with technology applications so that methods classes are closely aligned with the State Core Curricula in terms of technology use.
- Activity: Design teams will select eight education courses and four content methods courses in mathematics, English, science, and history, and design and implement curricula that will integrate technology into instruction.

Objective b: BYU courses will "support problem solving, data collection, information management, communications, presentations, and decision making" (NCATE Standard).

- Activity: Professors will assign technology projects to their pre-service teachers, thereby modeling infusion of technology for pre-service teachers.

Objective c: BYU courses will require students to "create multimedia presentations" (NCATE Standard).

- Activity: BYU cohort students will create electronic portfolios using multimedia software as part of their required courses.

Goal No. 3: BYU practica experiences will meet the NCATE Standards by providing opportunities for students to teach with technology.

Objective a: BYU students will "plan and deliver instructional units that integrate a variety of software applications and learning tools" (NCATE Standard).

- Activity: Pre-service teachers will implement at least one lesson plan in their practica experiences.

Objective b: BYU students will provide opportunities for collaboration with public school pupils in the use of technology.

- Activity: Pre-service teachers will link their students electronically with other classrooms that have BYU student teachers, especially those in Washington, D.C.

Goal No. 4: Pre-service teachers, cooperating teachers, and university faculty will become change agents (Fullan, 1993; Fullan, 1999) for the promotion of technology in the schools.

Objective a: BYU faculty will mentor colleagues in integrating technology into their curricula and in methods of working with pre-service teachers in their practical experiences.

- Activity: Summer institutes will provide opportunities for lessons learned about technology integration from one year to the next.
- Activity: Electronic networks of listserves will be created to share technology-rich curriculum.
- Activity: A BYU Web site will be designed to provide the networking of graduates from our teacher preparation program.

EVALUATION METHOD, DATA COLLECTION, AND DATA ANALYSIS

Internal and external evaluators have conducted a situated evaluation of the processes of personal and institutional change associated with the technology integration initiatives at BYU. Situated evaluation is a process-oriented approach and focuses on identifying the ways in which systemic reform and technology integration is often complexly realized in the lives and practices of individuals (Bruce, 1997; Bruce & Rubin, 1998). To trace the complex personal and institutional processes associated with learning to integrate technology, the evaluators developed case studies of curriculum design teams (Merriam, 1990). Case study data were collected during the three academic years of the grant. The data collected included detailed observations of the efforts of the PT3 support team related to the organization, support, and training of curriculum design teams; interviews with design team members; questionnaires from design team members; and an analysis of team products. The evaluators identified important principles associated with the organization and support of the curriculum design teams. The case study analysis demonstrates the ways in which the "curriculum design team model" facilitates systemic reform within the BYU School of Education and how these reforms reach affiliated schools and districts.

FACULTY DESIGN TEAMS

Year One: Development of Design Teams

When BYU was awarded a PT3 grant, a leadership team was formed. It consisted of a secondary education specialist, the associate chair of the Teacher Education Department (an elementary education specialist), an internal evaluator and instructional psychology specialist, a special assistant to the dean's office, and a technology specialist for the dean's office. The leadership team invited faculty involved in the teacher education program to begin to look at ways they could incorporate technology into their courses. Teams began to form around specific courses or other program activities. No two design teams had exactly the same structure or set of goals. The teams were allowed to define themselves as they began to participate in PT3 activities.

During the 2000-2001 academic year we began to implement the PT3 grant which, among other things, focused on developing curriculum design teams. BYU teacher education faculty and public school colleagues were invited to attend one- to two-day workshops focused on integrating technology into the K-12 curriculum and developing skills needed to use technology in instruction. Experts from Apple Computers, INTEL Teach to the Future, Casio, and the Utah Education Network were among the workshop facilitators. The ISTE standards were introduced. In addition, as a leadership team, we met with participants to discuss what they valued in their courses and how technology might enhance what they do. Design teams began to form as participants with common goals met at workshops focused on helping faculty integrate technology into their instruction.

Midway through the year we asked participants to define themselves into specific design teams by setting goals and contracting to accomplish them with PT3 funds. In the first year of the grant, eight design teams signed contracts. Each contract was unique in the support that would be offered and the goals that would be met, but they did have common activities. The teams agreed to attend additional workshops, meet regularly as a group, and attend a summer institute. The teams received funds to attend some of these activities, but only when they could show lesson plans, research presentations or papers, or student products that came as a result of PT3 participation. Members of three design teams presented their work at a national technology conference during the first year of the grant.

The summer institute was a culminating activity for the first year. The institute focused on two goals: portfolio development (with Helen Barrett, http://electronicportfolios.com/) and technology integration into the curriculum with examples from public school classrooms. Design teams were able to meet with other teams to discuss their uses of technology. They also met with the external evaluators for interviews about their work.

Year Two:
Developing Technology-Enhanced Teacher Education Curriculum

The most obvious change in PT3 activities the second year was the move away from outside presenters at workshops to presentations by design teams at monthly brown bags. Design teams shared ways in which they were integrating technology into their teacher education courses and presented student products. Pre-service teachers at BYU were creating educational portfolios and technology-enhanced K-12 curriculum. Four faculty members had attended an INTEL Teach to the Future workshop and were using the program in one elementary and two secondary education courses. As these products were being developed, design teams began to develop rubrics for evaluating the products based on the ISTE standards.

A unique activity during the second PT3 year was an excursion by many design team members to the Connected Classroom Conference in Las Vegas. This was organized and funded by the PT3 leadership team and designed to bring teacher education faculty, district personnel, and mentor teachers together to discuss technology and teacher education. There were organized activities prior to, during, and after the conference to facilitate alignment between the goals and practices within the McKay School of Education and within the participating schools and classrooms. Participants traveled in six BYU vans to the three-day technology conference. Design team members had set several goals prior to attending the conference. They attended many sessions as teams. This activity seemed to promote conversations about technology by participants in the vans based on the common experience of rethinking technology uses. The external evaluators wrote, "Not only did this event have the single greatest impact on faculty's perceptions, but also served as a powerful example of the serendipitous use of grant resources. This is clearly an excellent example of creative use of resources to promote long-term technology goals. At the time the grant was written this activity was not conceived; the grant leadership team saw this as an opportunity, strong interest in attending was expressed, the team organized the trip, and it was a great success. In retrospect this activity allowed for very important bonding to take place and enabled much of the superb work that has followed" (Connell & Johnson, 2002, p. 10).

Another new activity for design team members during the second year of the grant was to take the instructional technology course (IP&T 286) designed for pre-service teacher education candidates. This is a project-oriented lab course that familiarizes students with various kinds of instructional technologies through a series of tutorials. Additionally, there is a lecture component that focuses on issues of instructional design and technology integration. Taking this course helped participants become more aware of the kinds of technologies they could expect students to use in their course assignments. Participants mentioned that taking this course helped them better learn the technology skills presented to them and that they have found ways to better integrate those skills into their own courses and research. The traditional conference/workshop model opened their eyes to possible uses of technology, while the faculty-as-student model gave them the skills needed to produce technology-enhanced products, model those products, and write meaningful assignments for their students. Thirty-five (35) faculty members went through the IP&T 286 course. For the most part, these faculty members mentioned that the experience was extremely helpful. It was interesting to note that the appreciation for this experience seemed to boil down to one of two perspectives.

The first perspective tended to be expressed by the more technologically literate faculty and might be represented by the following statement made by one faculty member: "Now we have a much better idea of what the students coming to our classes have in terms of technology-related skills." This newfound awareness seemed helpful to many faculty to better gauge the level and intensity of the technology-based assignments required in their courses. Some faculty members felt that prior to this, students gave the impression that they had less in the way of technology skills than was actually the case. They felt that in some cases, students used a lack of technology skills as an excuse for not performing on assignments or for trying to talk their way out of assignments.

The second perspective could be associated with faculty who had traditionally avoided using technology and were in the process of acquiring new skills for themselves. One such faculty member said: "The IP&T 286 course that we went through was a great opportunity to learn some technology skills that I don't think I would have learned on my own." Of the course activities mentioned in particular were the many and varied tools and skills that the course enabled the faculty to master. One great benefit of this experience for some faculty was that they broadened the use of technology in their teaching.

Another opportunity provided by the PT3 grant was to attend the annual Society for Information Technology & Teacher Education (SITE) conference in Nashville, Tennessee. Twenty-three (23) people attended this conference (including faculty, clinical faculty, staff, and dean). The external evaluators stated that the strong presence of BYU's faculty at this conference did a great deal to advance BYU's reputation as a leader in the field of information technology in teacher education. Not only did attending this conference allow for exposure of the 23 attendees to national ideas and trends, but allowed faculty to publish and present their research findings at an international forum. In the minds of many faculty this served to legitimize their work. As one faculty member put it, "The grant provided an opportunity for me to participate in SITE, which was a wonderful experience. This gave me an opportunity to work and collaborate with different people and broadened my professional horizons."

The summer institute at the end of the second year introduced participants to WebQuests, an instructional process for integrating Internet research into problem-based learning. Design team members were encouraged to invite a public school teacher to a three-day workshop where they would work together to develop K-12 curriculum using WebQuests. They also created assignments for teacher education courses that would require BYU pre-service teachers to develop WebQuest K-12 lessons. The external evaluators reported that the 2002 summer institute, with its emphasis on WebQuests, was very positively received by faculty. This fact was brought forcefully home by one faculty member, "I think it's important during each institute that you actually are required to create a project while you are there. Otherwise things taper off and we never reach closure on anything."

Year Three: Moving Toward Sustainability

The third year of the grant saw the expansion of many of the design teams. The original eight teams had grown to at least fifteen. Some teams remained intact. Others split into more than one team as new members began to participate. More and more of the design teams began to work more deliberately with state and district specialists and classroom teachers. Their activities were focused on embedding technology permanently into teacher education courses with demonstrations, assignments, and accountability. Some teams began to expect technology lessons and activities from their students as they moved into a public school experience. Design team members joined statewide initiatives to link technology efforts in pre-service programs with mentoring and evaluation programs during the first and second year of teaching. The brown bags continued every month and a "Techie Talk" was added to teach the skills demonstrated during the brown bags. In the third year, 24 design team members attended the SITE technology conference and presented fifteen papers on the integration of technology into the BYU teacher education program.

The PT3 leadership team continued to focus on evaluation of the teacher education and K-12 curriculum being developed by faculty and students. We worked with selected design team participants to validate the rubric piloted in year two (Wentworth & Waddoups, 2002). Design teams members coded lessons created by their students. They reported that this helped them understand how lessons enhanced with Internet research and problem-solving supported high-level thinking more than lessons with technology production only. The final summer institute featured Dr. Christopher Moersch who presented his Levels of Technology Integration (LoTI) (see Dr. Moersch's Web site at http://k12. albemarle.org/MurrayElem/principal/doe99/techuse.html). LoTI has the same focus as the BYU PT3 grant, i.e., technology that enhances learning and teaching, not technology for its own sake. During this workshop design team participants were encouraged to evaluate the level of technology integration in their teacher education courses and in the products created by their pre-service teacher candidates. Our goal was to help the design teams evaluate their current level of technology use and have an evaluation tool as they move into a phase of technology implementation without PT3 support.

CONCLUSION

The articles in this collection tell the stories of the design teams and how they combined to establish systemic change in the McKay School of Education teacher education program. The next article presents six principles of change as established by the development of the teams, and in the following eight articles design team members share their involvement with PT3 activities, review their personal development, and discuss changes in their courses and products developed by their students. Articles three through eight are specific stories of the redevelopment of teacher education courses by the instructors who teach them. Articles nine and ten describe the process of changing a technology course required by the teacher education program. Article eleven discusses the process of extending the grant activities to our partnership school district and the State Office of Education. The final article describes a view of the BYU grant from the two external evaluators and how the work of the grant might be sustained without financial support. Our hope is to inform others engaged in the process of integrating technology into their teacher education programs.

REFERENCES

Bruce, B. C. (1997). Literacy technologies: What stance should we take? *Journal of Literacy Research, 29*(2), 289-309.

Bruce, B. C., & Rubin, A. (1998). *Electronic quills: A situated evaluation of using computers for writing in classrooms.* Hillsdale, NJ: Lawrence Erlbaum.

Connell, M., & Johnson, L. (2002). *External evaluator's report of BYU's PT3 Grant: Year two, 2001-2002.* Unpublished report.

Fullan, M. (1993). *Change forces: Probing the depths of educational reform.* London: The Falmer Press.

Fullan, M. (1999). *Change forces: The sequel.* London: The Falmer Press.

Jostens Learning Corporation. (1997, April 7). *Survey analysis by Global Strategy Group.* San Diego, CA: Author.

Kearsley, G. (1998). Educational technology: A critique. *Education Technology, 38*(2), 47-51.

Merriam, S. B. (1990). *Case study research in education: A qualitative approach.* San Francisco: Jossey-Bass.

Pappillion, M. L., & Cellitti, A. (1996). Developmental technology inservice training. *Technology and Teacher Education Annual.* Norfolk, VA: Association for the Advancement of Computing in Education, 427-430.

Riedl, J. (1995). *The integrated technology classroom: Building self-reliant learners.* Boston: Allyn & Bacon.

Ritchie, D., & Wilburg, K. (1994). Educational variables influencing technology integration. *Journal of Technology and Teacher Education, 2*(2), 143-153.

Strudler, N., Quinn, L., McKinney, M., & Jones, W. P. (1995). From coursework to the real world: First-year teachers and technology. *Technology and Teacher Education Annual.* Norfolk, VA: Association for the Advancement of Computing in Education, 774-777.

Wentworth, N. (1998). Technology inservice: A powerful change force. *Technology and Teacher Education Annual.* Norfolk, VA: Association for the Advancement of Computing in Education, 213-216.

Wentworth, N., & Waddoups, G. L. (July 2002). Systemic program redesign: The impact of PT3. Paper presented at the annual Preparing Tomorrow's Teachers to Use Technology (PT3) Conference, Washington, DC.

Willis, J., Willis, D., Austin, L. & Colón, B. (1995). Faculty perspectives on instructional technology: A national survey. *Technology and Teacher Education Annual.* Norfolk, VA: Association for the Advancement of Computing in Education, 795-800.

Gregory L. Waddoups
Nancy Wentworth
Rodney Earle

Principles of Technology Integration and Curriculum Development: A Faculty Design Team Approach

SUMMARY. To better prepare pre-service candidates for teaching in the information age, the International Society for Technology in Education (ISTE) has defined National Educational Technology Standards (NETS) to guide technology integration into teacher education programs. Based on these standards, Brigham Young University (BYU) has implemented strategies for technology integration into their teacher education program by creating curriculum design teams composed of School of Education faculty, public school personnel, and instructional design and technology specialists. This paper describes basic principles that have led to the successful development of curriculum design teams for systemic reform in teacher education. *[Article copies available for a fee from The Haworth Document Delivery Service: 1-800-HAWORTH. E-mail address:*

GREGORY L. WADDOUPS is Director, Instructional Design and Evaluation, The Center for Instructional Design, Brigham Young University, Provo, UT 84602 (E-mail: greg_waddoups@byu.edu).
NANCY WENTWORTH is Associate Professor, Department of Teacher Education, Brigham Young University, Provo, UT 84602 (E-mail: nancy_wentworth@byu.edu).
RODNEY EARLE is Professor and Associate Chair, Department of Teacher Education, Brigham Young University, Provo, UT 84602 (E-mail: rodney_earle@byu.edu).

[Haworth co-indexing entry note]: "Principles of Technology Integration and Curriculum Development: A Faculty Design Team Approach." Waddoups, Gregory L., Nancy Wentworth, and Rodney Earle. Co-published simultaneously in *Computers in the Schools* (The Haworth Press, Inc.) Vol. 21, No. 1/2, 2004, pp. 15-23; and: *Integrating Information Technology into the Teacher Education Curriculum: Process and Products of Change* (ed: Nancy Wentworth, Rodney Earle, and Michael L. Connell) The Haworth Press, Inc., 2004, pp. 15-23. Single or multiple copies of this article are available for a fee from The Haworth Document Delivery Service [1-800-HAWORTH, 9:00 a.m. - 5:00 p.m. (EST). E-mail address: docdelivery@haworthpress.com].

Digital Object Identifier: 10.1300/J025v21n01_02

<docdelivery@haworthpress.com> Website: <http://www.HaworthPress.com>

KEYWORDS. Systemic change, professional development

INTRODUCTION

Researchers, parents, and politicians have called for reform in K-12 education to include problem-based approaches to teaching and learning and the integration of learning technologies (Fullan & Stiegelbauer 1991; Means, 1994). Broadly, there have been two approaches to facilitate this systemic reform. One approach includes providing in-service training to practicing teachers designed to help them change their teaching practice (Fullan & Stiegelbauer, 1991). A second approach includes reforming pre-service education to include the use of learning technologies in the context of problem-based teaching and learning (Levin, Levin, & Waddoups, 1999). Both approaches require complex changes in people, processes, and support structures (Fullan & Stiegelbauer, 1991).

Connecting curriculum and technology is a goal of the McKay School of Education teacher preparation program. As part of the federal grant to prepare tomorrow's teachers to use technology, the McKay School of Education supported graduate and undergraduate students, technology specialists, public school teachers, and university faculty in a collaborative effort to create technology-enhanced curriculum. The key feature of these efforts was the development of faculty design teams which were organized and supported to create a technology-enhanced and problem-based curricula. The process of faculty change is often complex (Armstrong, 1996; Abbey, 1997; Candiotti & Clark, 1998), but is most successful in the context of robust support structures (Dusick, 1998). In this article, we report on the processes associated with organizing and supporting the faculty design teams.

Preparing tomorrow's teachers to integrate technology into their instruction requires university faculty to provide pre-service teachers with examples and experiences of learning enhanced with technology. To effectively accomplish this, teacher educators must adopt the knowledge, dispositions, and practices associated with effective technology integration. Successfully integrating technology into a teacher preparation program includes at a minimum rethinking the curriculum and methods of instruction; providing mentoring and support for associated faculty members; and developing collaborative relationships between and among faculty, students, schools districts, and beyond.

The technology integration model described here relies on the creation of curriculum design teams composed of school of education faculty, public school personnel, and instructional design and technology specialists. We will focus first on the definition of curriculum design teams and describe the principles associated with successful implementation of the design team model. If implemented properly, we believe the design team approach can provide faculty with motivation and support to engage in significant redesign activities that will lead to systemic and significant reform and technology integration.

CURRICULUM DESIGN TEAMS

Definition of Design Teams

Participants in curriculum design teams have defined the meaning of their participation in various ways. For example, one faculty member said: "A design team is a cooperative group working together to produce a unit of instruction. A design team creates an integrated curriculum task using technology that works." Another design team concluded: "A design team is a lot like a fashion consultant. The team members are involved in creating a product, reshaping and synthesizing this product, and, in many ways, creating a new fashion. To be a part of a design team means that you design and redesign." Yet another defined the design team as "a collaborative group working together and building a community." Six basic principles underlying the support and development of curriculum design teams and institutional change were identified (Waddoups, Wentworth, & Earle, 2003): *First*, early efforts must be made to understand the needs of key stakeholders involved in the teacher preparation program. *Second*, a core team, led by faculty must be organized and function to initiate the institutional change activities. *Third*, curriculum design teams should be organized according to naturally occurring alliances in the teacher education program and should build on the projects and interests of faculty members. *Fourth*, flexible support structures including access to instructional technologies and training must be provided to support the various needs and interests of teacher education faculty and design team members. *Fifth*, for curriculum design teams to be successful they must be committed to the idea of technology and systemic reform. *Sixth*, it is important to foster collaboration between and among curriculum design teams (Fullan & Stiegelbauer, 1991). We explain each of these principles in the context of the cases found in this volume.

Needs Analysis

The PT3 leadership team made early efforts to understand the needs of key stakeholders involved in the teacher preparation program. Meeting the needs of key stakeholders was crucial for the early success of the implementation of the portfolio design team. For example, they discovered from analysis of faculty responses to a questionnaire that there was a mismatch between faculty members' desires to integrate technology and their technology skills. This was apparent with the portfolio design team in their lack of knowledge with video editing software and their limited knowledge about portfolios in teacher education. Understanding this mismatch led to the selection of particular workshops and training opportunities that allowed them to learn important skills and dispositions that increased the quality of their projects.

Formal and informal interviews were conducted with each design team to determine how to best support their needs. For example, from interviews it became clear that design teams desired to present their redesign efforts at conferences. The PT3 leadership team adjusted the grant emphasis to fund design teams to present at conferences. Additionally, they found that they were interested in combining problem-based learning with technology integration. Using this information, the leadership team developed and delivered a week-long summer institute focusing on the use of WebQuests. This workshop was well attended, and many design teams are using WebQuests as part of their larger technology integration efforts.

Perhaps most important was the informal interviews and "hallway" conversations conducted by the leadership team. As colleagues, the leadership team learned about design team projects and gave encouragement to continue their efforts and advice on next steps. Many design teams mentioned the importance of this support to their work. This also provided valuable information about the support needs and how to organize the college-wide initiative.

To more systematically document progress, a yearly survey was given that tracked faculty members' technology usage and gathered information about the status of their design team work. These surveys were analyzed and used to provide training and support. For example, from the analysis of surveys after the first year of implementing the design team approach, many faculty expressed an interest in hearing about the work of other design teams. To meet this need, the leadership group developed "brown bags" and "tech-talks." On average 20 to 25 faculty members attended these meetings and in interviews reported that they were a source for inspiration. Additionally, the development of summer workshops and other support efforts were based on an analysis of conducting systematic needs analysis.

Faculty-Led Initiative

For college-wide curriculum design and technology integration efforts to be successful, they must be led by faculty. There is an important role for support organizations to provide resources, technical expertise, and instructional design expertise; however, faculty control and leadership are essential for giving legitimacy to these efforts.

Faculty members who are well respected by their colleagues led the PT3 leadership team and directed the technology integration activities. One leadership team member was a member of the elementary education faculty and an associate chair, and the other was a secondary education faculty member with technology integration experience and expertise. It has been important that these change efforts be seen as organic and originating from the faculty, rather than the academic administration. Indeed, faculty members occupied a unique place as mediators between administrators, students, and district support staff and as such were important change agents.

The two faculty members, one in elementary and one in secondary teacher education, involved in the PT3 grant were well respected among their colleagues and were seen as leaders. When the faculty design teams were interviewed, each spoke of the one-on-one consultation they received with these faculty members and the key role they played in furthering their technology integration efforts. Additionally, the faculty members involved in the grant have helped establish technology integration as an institutional agenda in the school of education through sitting on committees fostering technology integration. For example, one member of the grant team is a key member of the school of education electronic portfolio task force. As a leader on this task force and a participant on the PT3 grant, he was able to advocate for technology integration as an institutional goal. Faculty leadership has also been important to securing support for technology integration from the dean's office and from departments across the university.

The project leadership team worked behind the scenes to provide the various kinds of support needed for the success of the design teams. For example, one project leadership team member worked extensively with those involved in the development of electronic portfolios. Additionally, the project leadership team organized the summer institute, organized the Connected Classroom trip, and provided just-in-time assistance to many of the curriculum design teams. One of the big questions concerning the sustainability of these measures is the support of a leadership team after the life cycle of the grant.

Naturally Occurring Alliances

Curriculum design teams have been organized according to naturally occurring alliances in the teacher education program and have built on the projects and interests of faculty members. The portfolio design team consisted of teaching methods instructors, many of whom had worked together before the PT3 grant was received. Building on these alliances and relations, rather than constructing new ones, allowed for the integration activities to quickly develop. Portfolio design team members were already comfortable working together and were comfortable with their collaboration. Additionally, because they were both methods instructors and previously were teachers, they shared a great deal both personally and professionally. Other design teams were constructed around similar personal and institutional relationships which added to their success.

The WebQuest design team was organized because of several shared interests. First, they were all interested in the intersection of problem-based learning and technology integration and felt that WebQuests provided them with a unique opportunity to collaborate. Although the members of this team were not in the same discipline, they shared a commitment to providing their students with opportunities to integrate technology within the context of problem-based lessons. Working from these common goals, this team maintained a significant collaboration that will be sustained well beyond the grant's life. Each design team was successful in part because of common goals and organic connections they shared with respect to curriculum redesign and technology integration.

Flexible Support Structures

The integration activities associated with the PT3 grant provided flexible support structures, including access to instructional technologies and training and workshops. There was not a "one size fits all" approach to integration training. Each of the design teams, the port-folio design team, the WebQuest team, the secondary team, and the support and sustainability design team, received organized training on how to use particular technologies, on practices of technology integration, and on the uses and benefits of portfolios. In addition, they attended national conferences and workshops supported by the PT3 leadership team. They also received support to take the instructional technology course designed for their teacher education students. This support was systematic but flexible, allowing them to choose the support that best fit their needs. This formal support was comple-mented by informal support by the PT3 leadership team as well as support from other design teams and faculty. This less formal sup-port often occurred around the "brown bags" and "tech-talks," which have facilitated a culture of sharing and collaboration around issues of technology integration.

Personal Commitment to Redesign

The key to this curriculum design team's success was their personal and collective commitment to the idea of technology integration and systemic reform. The development of commitment came in two forms. First, each design team member was committed to one another as a team and, second, they were committed to the idea of technology integration as an institutional goal. In this way, they saw the possibilities of tech-nology in teacher education and developed a vision of these possibili-ties in their own teaching. In the experience of the portfolio design team, the vision was instilled through the formal training, summer in-stitutes, and sponsoring trips to conferences and workshops, and less formal brown bag talks. These professional development activities were organized around building relationships and developing deeper com-mitment to the idea of technology integration. During interviews with the WebQuest design team, it became clear that they shared both per-sonal and professional connections. They were familiar with other team members' efforts to use WebQuests and their successes and setbacks. Through working together, attending workshops, preparing presenta-tions, and traveling to conferences, they developed a personal commit-ment that continues to sustain their work.

Evidence for the portfolio design team's commitment included the members' desire to continue their technology integration efforts in the face of technical and institutional challenges. Even before their involve-ment in the PT3 grant, they demonstrated a willingness to persevere when times were difficult. They also demonstrated their commitment by presenting their electronic portfolio implementation to national conferences and to local audiences. Indeed, they are seen as leaders and pioneers within the McKay School in the area of technology integration and electronic portfolios in teacher education.

Collaboration Among Design Teams

It has been important to foster collaboration among curriculum design teams. It is only through this collaboration that systemic reform can take hold and lead to institutional change (Fullan & Stiegelbauer, 1991). We documented the collaboration within the portfolio design team and the widening reach of this group both within the teacher education program and beyond into schools, districts, and even statewide initiatives. As this group expanded its reach, other design teams in mathematics, science, history, language arts, and literacy began to see the value of electronic portfolios and to adopt their methods. This collaboration was fostered by formal presentations given by the portfolio team in the McKay School and less formal interactions in the hallway and during training sessions. Probably the most important outcome of this collaboration is a growing agreement among methods and content area faculty that a program-wide electronic portfolio would be both efficient and effective.

The WebQuest design team and the secondary cohort design team have begun to share their ideas about technology integration to other faculty members. Although it is early, there is evidence that other faculty are showing interest in the technology integration models developed by these two teams.

CONCLUSION

Taken together, these principles indicate that systemic reform is tantamount to cultural change. To change the culture of teaching and learning in pre-service preparation programs, the model must provide resources, rewards, well-thought-out experiences, and time for reflection. Through the cases discussed, the BYU PT3 model for integrating technology into the teacher education program demonstrated the ways in which curriculum design teams create a context of practice and reflection necessary for the personal and cultural changes desired to systemically reform the teacher education curriculum and integration of technology. Indeed, developing and fostering curriculum design teams create the possibility for wider scale change and sustainability over time. We also believe that these principles apply to professional development activities within school buildings and districts.

REFERENCES

Abbey, G. (1997). Developing a technology-friendly faculty in higher education. In D. Willis, B. Robin, J. Willis, L. Price, & S. McNeil (Eds.). *Technology and teacher education annual, 1997* (pp. 351-353). Charlottesville, VA: Association for the Advancement of Computing in Education.

Armstrong, G. (1996). One approach to motivating faculty to use multimedia. *T.H.E. Journal, 23*(10), 69-71.

Candiotti, A., & Clarke, N. (1998). Combining universal access with faculty development and academic facilities. *Communications of the ACM, 41*(1), 36-41.

Dusick, D. M. (1998). What social cognitive factors influence faculty members' use of computers for teaching? A literature review. *Journal of Research on Computing in Education, 31*(2), 21-36.

Fullan, M. G., & Stiegelbauer, S. (1991). *The new meaning of educational change* (2nd ed.). New York: Teachers School Press.

Levin, J., Levin, S. R., & Waddoups, G. (1999). Multiplicity in learning and teaching: A framework for developing innovative online education. *Journal of Research on Computing in Education, 32*(2), 256-269.

Means, B. (Ed.). (1994). *Technology and education reform: The reality behind the promise*. San Francisco: Jossey-Bass Publishers.

Waddoups, G. L., Wentworth, N., & Earle, R. (2003). Faculty learning to use technology: PT3 supported systemic reform initiatives in teacher education. *Educational Media and Technology Yearbook 2003*, pp. 198-204. Westport, CT: Libraries Unlimited.

Roni Jo Draper
Leigh Smith
Brenda Sabey

Supporting Change in Teacher Education: Using Technology as a Tool to Enhance Problem-Based Learning

SUMMARY. Sponsored by a *Preparing Tomorrow's Teachers to Use Technology* (PT3) grant, we participated in various activities designed to help us learn to infuse technology in our teacher education courses. The purpose of this paper is to describe the specific impact of the PT3 project activities on our change process–including the formation, evolution, and efforts of our curriculum design team–and to share the activities and products that we developed through participation in the grant activities. *[Article copies available for a fee from The Haworth Document Delivery Service: 1-800-HAWORTH. E-mail address: <docdelivery@haworthpress.com> Website: <http://www.HaworthPress.com> © 2004 by The Haworth Press, Inc. All rights reserved.]*

RONI JO DRAPER is Assistant Professor, Department of Teacher Education, Brigham Young University, Provo, UT 84602 (E-mail: roni_jo_draper@byu.edu).
LEIGH SMITH is Assistant Professor, Department of Teacher Education, Brigham Young University, Provo, UT 84602 (E-mail: leigh_smith@byu.edu).
BRENDA SABEY is Assistant Professor, Department of Teacher Education, Brigham Young University, Provo, UT 84602 (E-mail: brenda_sabey@byu.edu).

[Haworth co-indexing entry note]: "Supporting Change in Teacher Education: Using Technology as a Tool to Enhance Problem-Based Learning." Draper, Roni Jo, Leigh Smith, and Brenda Sabey. Co-published simultaneously in *Computers in the Schools* (The Haworth Press, Inc.) Vol. 21, No. 1/2, 2004, pp. 25-42; and: *Integrating Information Technology into the Teacher Education Curriculum: Process and Products of Change* (ed: Nancy Wentworth, Rodney Earle, and Michael L. Connell) The Haworth Press, Inc., 2004, pp. 25-42. Single or multiple copies of this article are available for a fee from The Haworth Document Delivery Service [1-800-HAWORTH, 9:00 a.m. - 5:00 p.m. (EST). E-mail address: docdelivery@haworthpress.com].

KEYWORDS. Technology, teacher education, reform, teacher development, problem-based learning

INTRODUCTION

Changing and improving education in the nation's schools has been a persistent focus of both private and government agencies for decades. Historically, this concern has led to wave after wave of reform initiatives, government mandates, and new programs aimed at restructuring both curriculum and instruction at various levels throughout the education system. Many of these efforts have targeted specific areas of the academic curriculum. For example, two major reform movements have dominated mathematics, science, and technology education throughout much of the 20th century (American Association for the Advancement of Science [AAAS], 1993; Deboer, 1991; Duschl, 1990; National Research Council [NRC], 1996), each in response to intense public criticism. More recently, attention has focused on the role of teacher education in the overall quality of schools and schooling in the United States, and the strident demand is for marked improvement and genuine reform in teaching, teacher education, teacher qualifications, and teacher quality (Cochran-Smith, 2001).

As a result of this concentrated interest and the associated demand for accountability in teacher education, significant resources have been allocated toward developing programs that enhance the impact of teacher education on teachers and teaching, particularly on teachers' ability to increase student learning (Cochran-Smith, 2003). The PT3 (Preparing Tomorrow's Teachers to Use Technology) grant project is a government-funded effort designed to encourage teacher preparation programs to integrate technology into teacher education courses in ways that help teachers understand how specific types of technology can be used to teach more effectively. Recipients are asked to support teacher educators as they learn ways to integrate technology in their university courses, modeling meaningful learning activities that prepare prospective teachers to use technology to improve student learning in their future classrooms. As with other funded efforts, the goal of PT3 is to change the way teacher educators and the teachers they prepare think about their instruction, altering what happens in their classrooms.

Changing practice, however, is a difficult endeavor. Although the history of education in the United States is replete with reform efforts at various levels, most of these have left very little lasting impact on classroom practices (Fullan, 1998; Sarason, 1990, 1996; Tyack & Tobin, 1994). There are a number of different explanations for this phenomenon (Woodbury & Gess-Newsome, 2002). However, it is generally agreed that classroom teachers–particularly their knowledge and beliefs about learning and instruction–play a fundamental role in mediating educational change (Fullan & Stiegelbauer, 1991; Putnam, Heaton, Prawat, & Remillard, 1992; Sarason, 1996). Indeed, it is ultimately the teacher who implements or fails to implement change. Successful reform, therefore, is largely dependent on teachers' ability to develop new knowledge and to alter existing beliefs about what it means to teach and to learn–a difficult process considering the resiliency of beliefs and belief systems (Pajares, 1992).

Despite individuals' tendency to hold fast to their beliefs about what it means to teach and to learn, it is possible to modify them. Change does occur in classroom practice. In order for this to occur, however, research suggests that existing beliefs must "prove unsatisfactory" (Gess-Newsome, Southerland, Johnston, & Woodbury, 2003; Pajares, 1992). It is only then that held beliefs can be altered or replaced. For teachers, "change requires dissatisfaction with the teaching and learning goals established for students, beliefs about students and how they learn, and beliefs about the effectiveness of instructional practices employed to meet newly established goals" (Gess-Newsome et al., 2003).

Research also suggests that context has a potentially powerful influence on teachers' beliefs about both academic content and pedagogy, as well as their ability or inclination to make changes in their practice (Bullough & Baughman, 1997; Lumpe, Haney, & Czerniak, 2000). Scholars (Cohen & Ball, 1990; Little, 1992; Sprinthall, Reiman, & Thies-Sprinthall, 1996) posit that the professional climate within which teachers work impacts their efforts to implement new practices–that teacher enthusiasm for professional development and change is greatest in institutions that make both formal and informal learning an integral part of teachers' work, and where that work is supported by colleagues and administration (Hopkins, 1990).

As teacher educators, it was some measure of dissatisfaction that prompted us to think differently about our own classroom instruction and ultimately led us to make changes in our practice. This process was also facilitated through the support of others. As relatively new faculty members, we actively participated in a number of learning experiences within our department that stimulated discussion and new ways of thinking about teaching and learning. Some of these experiences came as a result of project activities provided for us as part of a PT3 grant.

Others were a consequence of participation in a teacher education research/study group that was independently organized within our department. Still other experiences that prompted change were classroom interactions with students and were tied to the content that we, as teacher educators, are obligated to include in our methods courses based on various national standards documents.

This paper, however, describes only an excerpt from our continuing journey through the process of reflection and reformation of our practice. It focuses specifically on the influence of a systematic effort–funded by a PT3 grant–to help faculty members within the Department of Teacher Education at Brigham Young University improve their practice by integrating technology into their instruction. This reform effort was guided by six basic principles (see Waddoups, Wentworth, & Earle, 2003)–two of which were particularly critical to us as we began to develop different perspectives about teaching and learning in our classrooms. First, the PT3 leadership team encouraged us to organize curriculum design teams "according to naturally occurring alliances in the Teacher Education program" building on "the projects and interests of faculty members" (p. 199). Second, the leadership team provided "flexible support structures including access to instructional technologies and training . . . to support the various needs and interests of teacher education faculty" (p. 199). The purpose of this paper is to describe the specific impact of the PT3 project activities on our change process–including the formation, evolution, and efforts of our curriculum design team–and to share the activities and products that we developed through participation in the grant activities.

FORMING OUR CURRICULUM DESIGN TEAM

The PT3 leadership team, made up of faculty members from the Department of Teacher Education, invited other faculty members within the department and public school teachers from the BYU-Public School Partnership to participate in a number of teacher development activities (e.g., workshops and seminars) and to form curriculum design teams. These curriculum design teams (made up of small groups of university education faculty, content-specific methods teachers, cooperating public school personnel, or combinations of individuals from each of these groups) were organized by the PT3 leadership team in order for faculty members to support each other in their change efforts. Most teams were "organized according to naturally occurring alliances in the Teacher Education program" (Waddoups, Wentworth, & Earle, 2003, p. 199). Generally, this grouping was made according to disciplinary boundaries (e.g., science teacher educators teamed up with other science teacher educators, literacy educators with other literacy educators, and so forth). Therefore, for several months Draper and Sabey were part of the literacy education design team, while Smith participated with the science and mathematics education design team.

As time went by, however, several conditions or events combined to bring us together, abandoning our original groups and forming our own design team. First, as new faculty members in the department (Draper was in her second year, and Smith and Sabey had just begun their first year), we naturally sought each other out for support and friendship. Second, we had all joined a study group with a number of other colleagues in the department during which we read and discussed John Dewey's *Democracy and Education* (Dewey, 1916). The third event occurred when the coordinators of our institution's PT3 grant invited us to travel to Las Vegas, Nevada, for a Classroom Connect Conference to learn more about integrating technology into our classrooms. And finally, Smith and Sabey agreed to participate in a WebQuest design workshop, also sponsored by the PT3 grant.

During our reading and discussion of *Democracy and Education*, we individually began to examine the way we were teaching our classes, questioning our personal pedagogical choices: Did our own instruction match the kind of teaching we encouraged our prospective teachers to implement in their future classrooms? Were we effectively preparing our students with the knowledge and skills necessary to embrace the practices we described and claimed to espouse? Through conversations among colleagues in the study group, we came to two conclusions. First, we recognized that what we were promoting and what we were practicing were two contrasting methods of instruction. Having chosen a predominantly traditional, expository approach to teaching our methods courses, we served as poor models of the constructivist teacher we described and recommended that our prospective teachers become. Inquiry-based instruction was nearly absent from our classrooms, although we strongly encouraged our pre-service teachers to actively engage their students in authentic inquiry–even modeling learning activities they might use *with children*. These types of experiences were missing, however, from the learning activities that we planned for *our students* as they studied the methods of teaching literacy and science to children. Second, we recognized the complexities of teaching any given subject and the limitations of a single methods course in trying to adequately prepare beginning teachers for the classroom. At the same time, we understood that we each had a moral responsibility to help our pre-service teachers begin to make sense of the difficulties inherent in teaching so that they might approach their professional lives with children in informed, thoughtful, and just ways.

With these ideas swirling in our minds, we attended the Classroom Connect Conference (November 2001). We understood that the conference could potentially provide us with ideas for infusing technology into our methods classes. Because the conference was geared for public school teachers rather than teacher educators, however, there were few sessions that resonated with our new and developing aims. Instead, we spent much of the conference sitting in the conference hotel lobby discussing our courses, learning theories, and actions we might take to alter what was happening in our courses. We attended one session, however, wherein the presenter shared ideas about problem-based learning and briefly introduced us to WebQuests, as a technology-enhanced means of engaging students in inquiry. The ideas she offered fed our burgeoning desire to change our practice and suggested ways that we might accomplish our newly articulated goals. Additionally, the presentation led to new discussions about how we might find ways to integrate technology into our courses that would support students' learning and provide them with concrete examples of how to use technology to enhance their instruction. Ultimately, we began to question the current use of technology in our teacher education courses. We discovered that, in addition to our concerns about matching our pedagogy with the pedagogy we recommended and providing an adequate discipline-related preparation for our prospective teachers, we had begun to consider a new instructional issue: Could we include technology in our teaching in a way that would enhance our instruction, its impact on our students, and support our developing notions of how we should be teaching pre-service teachers, while modeling an effective use of technology in the elementary classroom?

Thus, when the coordinators of the PT3 grant invited members of the university faculty to participate in a WebQuest workshop, Smith and Sabey took advantage of the opportunity, assuming that WebQuests might provide a way to consider our three instructional dilemmas. The activities provided during the three-day workshop were designed to help participants develop a deeper understanding of WebQuests, including their purpose, construction, and evaluation, as well as how they might be used in both university and public school (K-12) instructional settings. Working in small groups, participants completed a WebQuest created by the PT3 leadership team as learners (in order to experience this type of Web-based learning activity) and worked through another WebQuest focused on criteria for developing and evaluating WebQuests (Dodge, 2002a). The final project was to create a WebQuest for actual use in either a K-12 classroom or for use with prospective teachers in an undergraduate methods course. The WebQuests that Smith and Sabey constructed (*http://www.byu.edu/ted/webquests.html*) were designed to introduce pre-service teachers to vocabulary, issues, and concepts that are relevant to the fields of science and literacy education for elementary children.

It was at this point that we each decided to abandon our original curriculum design teams and approached the PT3 leadership team with our desire to work together as a curriculum design team based on our common goals and assumptions about teaching and learning. We assumed that a case would have had to be made to the leadership team based on our different content areas (Smith, science, and Sabey and Draper, literacy) and the different populations we served (Smith and Sabey, elementary, and Draper, secondary). However, the leadership team enthusiastically supported our decision.

Soon, we had grown into various roles as members of our new curriculum design team–roles that emerged as we worked collaboratively to make changes in our individual practices. After creating the WebQuests, Smith and Sabey implemented them in their undergraduate methods courses; Smith in her science methods course and Sabey in her literacy methods course. Meanwhile, Draper served as a critical friend during the implementation of the WebQuests in Smith's and Sabey's courses, reviewing and offering suggestions as the WebQuests were created, even checking the appropriateness of Internet sites chosen by Sabey for the literacy WebQuests. Once students had completed the WebQuests and created and presented the products associated with them (graphic organizers), Draper then sat with Smith and Sabey on separate occasions to check the students' work against the content and pedagogical standards associated with science and literacy teaching. Later in the semester, after the students in each of the methods courses had worked together in small groups to construct WebQuests of their own, these products were also shared, allowing each member of our curriculum design team to evaluate the content and format for accuracy and appropriateness.

ACTIVITIES OF OUR CURRICULUM DESIGN TEAM

By the time we had formed our team, we had a clear sense of the three issues we wanted to face together: (a) to base our instruction on current learning theory and research-based practices, which are those we would want our students to implement with public school children; (b) to confront the task of providing our students with sufficient knowledge and appropriate skills needed for teaching and solving instructional problems given the limited time allocated to a single methods course; and (c) to prepare pre-service teachers for the integration of technology in their classrooms.

To address the first two of these issues, we adopted a problem-based learning/teaching model in our science and literacy elementary education methods courses. Problem-based learning and teaching is understood to be a model that engages individuals in a process of learning by examining problems connected to real life and finding meaningful solutions (Delisle, 1997; Duch, Groh, & Allen, 2001). We chose this model because it honors a constructivist approach to learning and cognition by helping students to strengthen their understanding and construct knowledge as they create solutions to complex problems–allowing us to model appropriate teaching methods. We introduced problems to students that resembled the kinds of problems they would likely face in their future classrooms as elementary science and literacy teachers. Students then worked in cooperative groups, using various professional resources (e.g., journals, books, Internet sites, field professionals) to seek and develop possible solutions to the posed problems. Finally, students shared the solutions prepared by the groups with the entire class and the cycle continued with a new problem. We looked to problem-based learning to help us provide learning opportunities that would help our students construct the knowledge, skills, and dispositions needed for teaching within the limited time frame of one semester.

While our adoption of problem-based learning addressed the first two issues, the third issue, technology integration, required us to find additional assistance. The PT3 leadership team provided that support. They accomplished this by providing both general support (appropriate for any faculty in the Department of Teacher Education) and specific support (aimed specifically at our curriculum design team). The leadership team provided funding for us to attend conferences, both as learners and presenters; they prepared workshops on various technology options; they planned opportunities for sharing the work of professors who were exploring the integration of technology into their classes; and they offered more informal support through encouragement, advice, and praise.

As we examined our efforts to integrate technology with our content instruction (methods and strategies of teaching science or literacy to elementary children, and the pedagogical, social, and political issues related to the possible alternatives) and to prepare our students to effectively use technology in their teaching, we sought learning activities or methodologies that would engage students in the process of problem solving while requiring them to utilize available technology. We selected the use of WebQuests as learning tools in our methods courses because they have been described as a means of promoting problem-solving skills. A WebQuest is "an inquiry-oriented activity in which some or all of the information that learners interact with comes from resources on the Internet" (Dodge, 1995) and may be either "short-term" (requiring one to three days to complete) or "long-term" (typically taking from one to four weeks or more) (Schrock, 2002). Dodge, the originator of the WebQuest idea, asserts that WebQuests help students "focus on using information" and "support learners' thinking at the levels of analysis, synthesis and evaluation" (cited in Arthur, n.d., 2). Additionally, as a directed Web search, the teacher (a) becomes acquainted with the sites students will use, (b) ensures that each site is safe and of high quality, and (c) saves instructional time, focusing on the research or problem solving rather than spending learning time searching for information (Arthur, n.d.).

Although we chose to include WebQuest activities in each of our courses as a viable way to enhance our problem-based learning environment, the way these Web-based inquiry activities were used varied. These variations were necessary given the differing content and contexts of our courses (science methods and literacy methods classes). In the following section, we will briefly describe how WebQuests were used in each of the methods courses.

Science Methods Course

Smith used WebQuests in her science methods course in two ways: (a) to introduce students to the content of the course and (b) to allow students to create their own WebQuests for use with elementary-aged students. First, Smith created a WebQuest (*http://www.byu.edu/ted/webquests.html*) designed to provide the pre-service teachers with an overview of the appropriate information and skills they should acquire as they begin to think about teaching science–those topics and issues that would be examined more closely throughout the semester. The 21 prospective teachers in the class were asked to work collaboratively in teams of three to examine 15 specific Web sites selected by the instructor in order to answer the following questions: (a) What is involved in teaching science in elementary schools? and (b) What do you need to know about science and science instruction to provide children with quality science learning experiences? After exploring the Web-based literature, each team was then required to create a graphic organizer of their choice (using Microsoft Word, Inspiration, or other appropriate software), illustrating what they had identified to be the key issues involved in acquiring an understanding of science education in the elementary schools and teaching science effectively to children and the relationships between each of these topics.

Later in the semester, Smith required her students to create their own WebQuests. For this assignment, students explored how they might engage elementary children in meaningful inquiry-based science activities using technology in their future classrooms. In order to accomplish this, the students were first introduced to a sampling of the multiple resources available to help teachers and students construct Web-based learning tasks that promote critical thinking and problem solving (Dodge, 2002b; March 2002)–skills and abilities that are emphasized in current science standards documents (AAAS, 1993; NRC, 1996). Smith then asked students to work in small groups (three to four students) to work cooperatively to create a content-based inquiry lesson or Web-based science learning activity in the form of a WebQuest appropriate for elementary-age students (*http://www.byu.edu/ted/webquests.html*).

Literacy Methods Course

In the literacy methods course, Sabey also used WebQuests in two ways: (a) to expose students to the content of the course and (b) to allow students to create their own WebQuests for their peers to further explore issues related to literacy instruction. Sabey created the first WebQuest (*http://www.byu.edu/ted/webquests.html*) with the purpose to deepen her students' understanding of Balanced Literacy Instruction in the intermediate grades. She required students to complete four tasks, each building on the previous task to answer the question: What does Balanced Literacy Instruction look like in an intermediate grades classroom? They worked in teams of three and examined multiple Web sites and other media sources (CDs) to complete the following tasks:

> Task 1–Create a graphic organizer illustrating the components of a Balanced Literacy program.
> Task 2–Create a balanced literacy classroom map and daily schedule.
> Task 3–Create an E-File of literacy strategies. Use this informa-

tion in constructing a chart of activities aligned with the sixth-grade language arts state core curriculum standards and Balanced Literacy components.

Task 4–Plan lesson plans for one day's literacy lessons in a Balanced Literacy classroom. Use one of the sixth-grade language arts state core curriculum standards listed in Task 3.

The goal of the second WebQuest experience, created by the students, was twofold: (a) to provide an opportunity for students to learn pedagogical content knowledge related to teaching literacy skills and (b) to allow students to experience the use of WebQuests as an instructional tool. First, the students were asked to work in groups and create a WebQuest based on questions that arose in their four-week field experience. Upon returning to campus from the field, the students created a list of questions that were sorted into categories. They included six topic areas: comprehension, diversity of learners, spelling, writing, motivation, and phonics/phonemic awareness. The students broke into groups of three to four and chose a topic area they wanted to research. Each group created a WebQuest (*http://www.byu.edu/ted/webquests. html*) that would answer their questions and teach their peers about their topic. The guidelines for the student-created WebQuests required that the problems be based on a real-life context, involve higher order thinking, and, because of time constraints, take approximately one hour to complete.

The second part of the student-generated WebQuest assignment required the students to complete one another's WebQuests. Examples of the tasks included modifying a shared reading lesson for diverse learners, creating a lesson plan focusing on one comprehension thinking strategy, writing a philosophy for teaching spelling, or responding to a classroom scenario related to motivating students. Time in class was used to discuss what they were learning as they completed the Web-based inquiry created by their peers.

While we were pleased with what the students were able to accomplish with the use of the WebQuests, we were concerned about some aspects of the experience. First, the amount of time it required to prepare the students to create their own WebQuests was more than we had anticipated. Because this type of learning activity was new to virtually all of our pre-service teachers, it was necessary to guide them through a process of learning all about WebQuests–allowing time for them to experience a WebQuest as learners, teaching them the purpose and characteristics of an effective WebQuest, and evaluating WebQuests as a guided, Web-based teaching/learning tool. As we had limited time for our classes to begin with, the time needed to teach the students about the technology of WebQuests reduced the time for their learning of content (science and literacy pedagogy). We shared this concern with the leadership team and with the individuals responsible for the technology courses for the teacher education program. As a result of those conversations, WebQuests are now introduced in the initial technology course in the teacher education program.

Second, we were concerned that the WebQuests were too structured to provide the kind of flexibility students needed during their problem-solving activities. However, due to our students' lack of experience in problem-based learning, we altered our thinking about the amount of structure provided in a WebQuest. We came to see WebQuests as a way to guide and to support the students through the problem-solving process and to prepare them for less structured problem-solving activities, thus providing a more successful learning experience. Furthermore, the WebQuests provided a context for discussing inquiry-based teaching and the importance of the problem in guiding the inquiry. Therefore, rather than detracting from problem-based learning, the WebQuests provided a scaffolded inquiry experience for our students and the context necessary for them to discuss issues related to problem-based/inquiry-based teaching methods with greater complexity. Indeed, we felt confident that WebQuests would successfully assist us in matching our instruction with current theories of pedagogy, providing our students with sufficient content and pedagogical knowledge (along with a familiarity with the multiple resources available to continue to support them as they begin teaching), and integrating technology in our science and literacy methods courses.

Studying Our Activities

With some encouragement from the PT3 leadership team, we decided to study the effectiveness of WebQuests as instructional tools in our methods courses and to explore the usefulness of using WebQuests to prepare teachers to integrate technology in their classrooms. This research was important not only to inform our own practice, but also to inform the field. The use of WebQuests to teach and integrate academic content at all grade levels (Abruscato, 2000; Watson, 1999; Yoder, 1999) has been well documented. However, there is little empirical data describing their impact on student learning, and minimal evidence that these types of learning activities have been used in teacher education methods courses to teach pedagogy.

We collected qualitative data to seek answers to these questions (Bogdan & Biklen, 1998; Jacob, 1992). Data sources included (a) student questionnaires, (b) teaching journals (kept by the course instructors), (c) student and teacher artifacts (including WebQuests created by the teachers and those created by the students), and (d) course evaluations. The data were analyzed using national science, literacy, and technology standards for teachers as analytical frameworks (International Reading Association [IRA], 2000; International Society for Technology in Education [ISTE], 2000; NRC, 1996).

We found that the use of WebQuests enabled us to attend to the three issues we faced in preparing teachers for elementary classrooms. As we indicated earlier, the choice of a problem-based approach to teaching and learning (using WebQuests as one of multiple instructional tools) helped us base our instruction on current learning theory (Bransford, Brown, & Cocking, 2000) and research-based practices (Cambourne, 2002; NRC, 1996), which are those we would want our students to implement with public school children. Furthermore, the results of our analysis indicate that the use of WebQuests in methods courses were (a) useful to help students gain requisite knowledge and skills for teaching elementary science and literacy and (b) supported technology integration in ways that modeled for our students how they might integrate technology in their classrooms.

Sharing Our Findings

The leadership team encouraged us to share our experience and findings with others. Through informal discussions with the leadership team we were able to identify several appropriate avenues. First, we presented our results at two professional conferences: The University of Nevada, Reno, Technology Symposium: Putting the Pieces Together (November 2002); and the 15th Annual International Conference of the Society for Information Technology and Teacher Education (SITE) in Albuquerque, New Mexico (March 2003). In both cases, we gained a greater understanding of our own efforts to use technology to enhance instruction and the work of others in the field of technology and education. Following these presentations, the leadership team encouraged us to further publicize our experiences. As a result, we wrote and submitted a research article for publication.

Plans for Future Activities

Because of the success of our using WebQuests and inasmuch as our data analysis revealed that we needed to make some adjustments in how we implemented WebQuests in our courses, we have made plans to continue our work together as a design team. As a team, we have applied for, and been awarded, a grant from the university's Center for Instructional Design. We are planning to create a Web site to support our students in their problem-based learning and their creation and use of instructional tools that support inquiry-based teaching/learning, such as WebQuests. The site will primarily support our students as they engage in course assignments; however, we hope to make the site useful to others (i.e., students, practitioners, public-school faculty, and university faculty) interested in problem-based learning and WebQuests. Additionally, having implemented WebQuests with our undergraduate students, we are exploring the extension of using WebQuests with our graduate students. We recognize the potential of guided Web-based activities to provide support for our graduate students in seminar or independent study courses. Finally, as we continue to refine our efforts in using WebQuests and other technology-enhanced learning experiences in problem-based learning, we acknowledge the need for continued examination of their effectiveness.

CONCLUSIONS

Our shared beliefs, and thus our shared dissatisfactions (Gess-Newsome et al., 2003; Pajares, 1992), prompted us to engage in activities that would help us make meaningful changes in our individual practices. Our activities were similar, in many ways, to those of practicing K-12 teachers who might also seek changes within their own practice. Indeed, our experience was not unlike Dickinson, Burns, Hagen, and Locker (1997) who described their efforts, as four first-grade teachers, to improve their teaching of science. Together, they were able to (a) recognize and become committed to the fact that they needed to change their practice, (b) discuss and reflect on their practice as they tried new ways of thinking about teaching and learning science, and (c) receive support from one another, as well as others outside their group, as they continued to develop their teaching practices. The support we received came both from structures we sought out and/or created for ourselves (e.g., the discussion of Dewey) and from support structures like those provided by the PT3 leadership team (e.g., seminars and workshops). In fact, the framework for change embraced by the PT3 leadership team was based on their understanding of principles necessary to support design teams and institutional change (Waddoups, Wentworth, & Earle, 2003). Their efforts acknowledged and supported our need to work together as a team, despite the fact that we had disparate foci within the department of teacher education. Furthermore, the variety and flexibility of support (e.g., workshops, one-to-one consultation) provided by the PT3 leadership team allowed us to engage in the activities that best matched our interests and needs.

The leadership team worked to help us, as teacher educators, to integrate technology in our classrooms in a way that modeled effective technology implementation and helped our pre-service teachers to think about their future use of technology to enhance learning. While this aspect of change was never part of our early conversations together as collaborative colleagues, issues of instructional technology did creep into our view as a result of our inclusion in the activities prepared by the PT3 leadership team. For instance, we would not have sought out a technology conference to attend, especially one geared primarily for K-12 teachers. However, due to the invitation of the leadership team and the support the team had from our department chair, we agreed to attend the conference. And while there were few sessions focused on teacher preparation, the conference did provide us with time to continue conversations about learning, teaching, and preparing teachers–time that is often scarce during our regularly scheduled, frazzled work weeks. Furthermore, the conference served as a catalyst for further discussions of problem-based learning and even provided an idea of how technology might serve as a solution to some of the concerns we faced in our classrooms.

We have not resolved all of our issues nor answered all of our questions regarding learning, teaching, and preparing teachers. Thus, our work together as a design team or professional development team will continue beyond the life of the PT3 grant. We suspect that we will continue to look to technology to help us resolve the issues we face in teacher education, but we expect that we will continue to consider problems and issues first and seek out technology later. In fact, we believe that the success we have found in the use of technology in our pre-service courses is due to our reluctance to simply employ technology for technology's sake. Rather, we carefully considered the potential of technology to address pedagogical issues. We believe that technology instruction in schools is necessary so students can gain a greater knowledge of the world, their community, and how to address and solve the problems they face as participants in a community. Our hope for pre-service teachers is that they will consider the potential power of technology to transform the way children and young people learn.

REFERENCES

Abruscato, J. (2000). *Teaching children science: A discovery approach.* Boston: Allyn & Bacon.

American Association for the Advancement of Science (AAAS). (1993). *Benchmarks for science literacy.* New York: Oxford University Press.

Arthur, P. (n.d.). Retrieved October 9, 2002, from http://sesd.sk.ca/teacherresource/802/WebQuesthandout.htm

Bogdan, R. C., & Biklen, S. K. (1998). *Qualitative research for education: An introduction to theory and methods.* Boston: Allyn & Bacon.

Bransford, J. D., Brown, A. L., & Cocking, R. R. (Eds.) (2000). *How people learn: Brain, mind, experience, and school.* Washington, DC: National Academy Press.

Bullough, R. V., & Baughman, K. (1997). *"First-year teacher" eight years later: An inquiry into teacher development.* New York: Teachers College Press.

Cambourne, B. (2002). Holistic, integrated approaches to reading and language arts instruction: The constructivist framework of instructional theory. In A. E. Farstrup & S. J. Samuels (Eds.), *What research has to say about reading instruction* (3rd ed., pp. 25-47). Newark, DE: International Reading Association.

Cochran-Smith, M. (2001). Desperately seeking solutions. *Journal of Teacher Education, 52*(5), 347-349.

Cochran-Smith, M. (2003). Assessing assessment in teacher education. *Journal of Teacher Education, 54*(3), 187-191.

Cohen, D., & Ball, D. (1990). Policy and practice: An overview. *Educational Evaluation and Policy Analysis, 12*(3), 233-239.

Deboer, G. E. (1991). *A history of ideas in science education: Implications for practice.* New York: Teachers College Press.

Delisle, R. (1997). *How to use problem-based learning in the classroom.* Alexandria, VA: Association for Supervision and Curriculum Development.

Dewey, J. (1916). *Democracy and education.* New York: The Macmillan Company.

Dickinson, V. L., Burns, J., Hagen, E. R., & Locker, K. M. (1997). Becoming better primary science teachers: A description of our journey. *Journal of Science Teacher Education, 8*(4), 295-311.

Dodge, B. (1997, May 5). *Some thoughts about WebQuests.* Retrieved October 9, 2002, from http://edweb.sdsu.edu/courses/edtec596/about_webquests.html

Dodge, B. (2002a). *A WebQuest about WebQuests.* Retrieved July 10, 2002, from http://webquest.sdsu.edu/webquestwebquest-es.html

Dodge, B. (2002b). *The WebQuest page at San Diego State University.* Retrieved July 10, 2002, from http://webquest.sdsu.edu

Duch, B. J., Groh, S. E., & Allen, D. E. (2001). *The power of problem-based learning: A practical "how to" for teaching undergraduate courses in any discipline.* Sterling, VA: Stylus.

Duschl, R. A. (1990). *Restructuring science education: The importance of theories and their development.* New York: Teachers College Press.

Fullan, M. (1998). The meaning of educational change: A quarter century of learning. In D. Hopkins (Ed.), *The international handbook of educational change* (pp. 214-228). Boston: Kluwer.

Fullan, M., & Stiegelbauer, S. (1991). *The new meaning of educational change.* New York: Teachers College Press.

Gess-Newsome, J., Southerland, S. A., Johnston, A., & Woodbury, S. (2003). Educational reform, personal practical theories, and dissatisfaction: The anatomy of change in college science teaching. *American Educational Research Journal, 40*(3), 731-767.

Hopkins, D. (1990). Integrating staff development and school improvement: A study of personality and school climate. In B. Joyce (Ed.), *ASCD Yearbook: Changing school culture through staff development* (pp. 41-67). Alexandria, VA: Association for Supervision and Curriculum Development.

International Reading Association (2000). *Standards for reading professionals.* Newark, DE: Author.

International Society for Technology in Education (2000). *National educational technology standards for teachers.* Eugene, OR: Author.

Jacob, E. (1992). Culture, context, and cognition. In M. D. LeCompte, W. L. Millroy, & J. Preissle (Eds.), *The handbook of qualitative research in education* (pp. 293-335). New York: Academic Press.

Little, J. (1992). Teacher development and educational policy. In M. Fullan & A. Hargreaves (Eds.), *Teacher development and educational change* (pp. 170-193). Bristol, PA: Falmer.

Lumpe, A. T., Haney, J. J., & Czerniak, C. M. (2000). Assessing teachers' beliefs about their science teaching context. *Journal of Research in Science Teaching, 37*(3), 275-292.

March, T. (2002, August 1). *Why WebQuests? An introduction.* Retrieved October 9, 2002, from http://ozline.com/webquests/intro.html

National Research Council (NRC). (1996). *National science education standards.* Washington, DC: National Academy Press.

Pajares, M. F. (1992). Teachers' beliefs and educational research: Cleaning up a messy construct. *Review of Educational Research, 62*(3), 307-322.

Putnam, R. T., Heaton, R. M., Prawat, R. S., & Remillard, J. (1992). Teaching mathematics for understanding: Discussing case studies of four fifth-grade teachers. *The Elementary School Journal, 93*(2), 213-229.

Sarason, S. B. (1990). *The predictable failure of educational reform: Can we change course before it's too late?* San Francisco: Jossey-Bass.

Sarason, S. B. (1996). *Revisiting "The culture of the school and the problem of change."* New York: Teachers College Press.

Schrock, K. (2002). *WebQuests in our future: The teacher's role in cyberspace.* Retrieved October 9, 2002, from http://school.discovery.com/schrockguide/webquest/webquest.html

Sprinthall, N. A., Reiman, A. J., & Thies-Sprinthall, L. (1996). Teacher professional development. In J. Sikula (Ed.), *Handbook of research on teacher education* (pp. 666-703). New York: Simon & Schuster Macmillan.

Tyack, D., & Tobin, W. (1994). The "grammar" of schooling: Why has it been so hard to change? *American Educational Research Journal, 31*(3), 453-479.

Waddoups, G. L., Wentworth, N., & Earle, R. (2003). Faculty learning to use technology: PT3-supported systemic reform initiative in teacher education. In M. A. Fitzgerald, M. Orey, & R. M. Branch (Eds.), *Educational media and technology yearbook 2003* (pp. 198-204). Westport, CT: Libraries Unlimited.

Watson, K. L. (1999, July). Webquests in the middle school curriculum: Promoting technological literacy in the classroom. *Meridian: A Middle School Computer Technologies Journal, 2*(2). Retrieved October 9, 2002, from http://www.ncsu.edu/meridian/jul99/webquest/index.html

Woodbury, S., & Gess-Newsome, J. (2002). Overcoming the paradox of change without difference: A model of change in the arena of fundamental school reform. *Educational Policy, 16*, 763-782.

Yoder, M. B. (1999, April). The student WebQuest. *Learning and Leading with Technology, 26*(7). Retrieved October 9, 2002, from http://www.iste.org/L&L/26/7/features/yoder/index.html

J. Merrell Hansen
Nancy Nalder-Godfrey

The Power of Action Research, Technology and Teacher Education

SUMMARY. This study is a review of a program and an endeavor that sought to examine the effects of preparing prospective teachers in the skills and abilities of action research, utilizing technological resources, and determining the impact of that upon teacher education efforts. A cohort of secondary student teachers were taught and prepared in the processes and activities associated with action research, a means of identifying one's own issues and concerns with teaching and conducting a valuable study and examination of those issues. They were asked to organize, prepare, present, and evaluate their research activities by utilizing technology and demonstrating these results. Finally, they were asked to evaluate the implications that this effort had on their teacher education program and professional development. *[Article copies available for a fee from The Haworth Document Delivery Service: 1-800-HAWORTH. E-mail address: <docdelivery@haworthpress. com> Website: <http://www.HaworthPress.com> © 2004 by The Haworth Press, Inc. All rights reserved.]*

J. MERRELL HANSEN is Professor, Department of Teacher Education, Brigham Young University, Provo, UT 84602 (E-mail: merrell_hansen@byu.edu).
NANCY NALDER-GODFREY is a graduate student at Towson University, and a teaching intern at Garrison Forest School, Owings Mills, MD 21117 (E-mail: naldergodfrey@yahoo.com).

[Haworth co-indexing entry note]: "The Power of Action Research, Technology and Teacher Education." Hansen, J. Merrell, and Nancy Nalder-Godfrey. Co-published simultaneously in *Computers in the Schools* (The Haworth Press, Inc.) Vol. 21, No. 1/2, 2004, pp. 43-57; and: *Integrating Information Technology into the Teacher Education Curriculum: Process and Products of Change* (ed: Nancy Wentworth, Rodney Earle, and Michael L. Connell) The Haworth Press, Inc., 2004, pp. 43-57. Single or multiple copies of this article are available for a fee from The Haworth Document Delivery Service [1-800-HAWORTH, 9:00 a.m. - 5:00 p.m. (EST). E-mail address: docdelivery@haworthpress.com].

http://www.haworthpress.com/web/CITS
© 2004 by The Haworth Press, Inc. All rights reserved.
Digital Object Identifier: 10.1300/J025v21n01_04

KEYWORDS. Action research, teacher education, school-based decision making, professional development, technology applications, professional inquiry

INTRODUCTION

Jacob Bronowski, noted for his insightful and thoughtful analysis of the human condition, commented on the evolution and revolution in the way we think and learn. Bronowski was a personal colleague and associate of several individuals who were involved in some of the most dramatic and critical mathematical and physics developments of the 20th century, including the Manhattan Project. He wrote:

> There is one gift above all others that makes man unique among the animals, and it is the gift displayed everywhere: his immense pleasure in exercising and pushing forward his own skill. . . . The most powerful drive in the ascent of man is his pleasure in his own skill. He loves to do what he does well and, having done it well, he loves to do it better. (Bronowski, 1973, pp. 113, 116)

This well could describe teaching and teachers. There is a lifetime obsession of teachings to improve their practices and enhance their results. The aspiration of all is that they will be effective and efficient teachers, encouraging young students to learn and master the skills and knowledge necessary to prepare them for life. This motivates and inspires teachers throughout their careers and seems to help them survive discouragement and frustrations inherent in the profession.

Yet, realistically and pragmatically, the routine, the endless demands, and the unexpected crises make teaching one of the most complex of human enterprises. Teachers seem to be locked into self-contained realms, frequently nothing more than their own classrooms that become their professional lives. It is this exact scenario that prevents teachers from encouraging change, particularly in relationship to technology. They have a system that works. It is tried and true. And if it works, why fix it? Advocates have called for change and reform to reduce this intellectually and professionally confining culture: "It is time to end the era of solo teaching in isolated classrooms. Good teaching thrives in a supportive learning environment created by teachers and school leaders who work together to improve learning–in short, quality teaching requires strong, professional learning communities" (Hunt & Carroll,

2003, p. 17). Heraclitus, the Greek philosopher, said it appropriately, "change alone is unchanging."

THE NEED FOR A CRITICAL STUDY OF ONE'S OWN CLASSROOM

Following the advice of Bronowski that we inherently seek to improve our skills and competencies and the admonition to seek out professional learning communities, teachers are asked to consider a new schema of thinking about what they do and how they learn about their own practices. Traditionally, teachers relied upon outside researchers and scholars to study and learn about schools and teaching. However, these outside experts seemed more intent on finding conclusions that resulted in little change or improvement in the actual classroom. Teachers were studied but were not improved by the process.

A newer concept about professional development is now being advocated. This is markedly different from the traditional and conventional practices alluded to previously. This means changing the "intellectual environment in which teachers work" (Wineburg & Grossman, 1998, p. 350). Such a learning community exists where learners learn from their own practices and where improvement occurs because of their own experiences. The advocacy of creating a learning community has significant impact upon the individual teacher and a school as a teaching/learning culture. A critical source of this enrichment and renewal is the introspective and reflective nature of teachers and educators that is present within their own classrooms and schools. They are the agents for understanding and they acquire the reason for professional growth.

> The focus on teacher development, the creation of curriculum leadership roles, the development of peer coaching schemes, the introduction of mentor programs, experiments with collaborative planning, and the growth of school-based management and decision-making all provide testimony to the ways in which many schools and school systems are seeking to involve teachers more in the life and work of the school outside the classroom, to have them take responsibility for the policies and practices that are created there. (Fullan & Hargreaves, 1996, p. 2)

A significant number of individuals are realizing the importance and value of teachers studying their own practices in order to be the energy force for change. For example, Cole and Knowles (2000) noted that we should see "teaching as inquiry." It is "researching" done by teachers for teachers.

> This view is counter to traditional notions of research on teaching, which typically conjure up images of professional researchers (perhaps white-coated, clinical, and usually university-based)– "outsiders" with little experience or context-based understanding of classroom and teaching life, at least from a teacher's perspective–conducting scientifically controlled investigations primarily for academic or pseudopractical purposes. (Cole & Knowles, 2000, p. 1)

DEFINING ACTION RESEARCH

There is a significant challenge for teachers to become students of their own practices. Action research personalizes and prioritizes what teachers learn because the research has an impact on teacher practices. Although teachers have not been prepared nor encouraged to do it, this kind of research has implications for improving the instructional process and enhancing the professional changes in the school and system. As other professions methodically consider their own work, it is imperative now that teachers and educators do similarly. The consequences are filled with substantial promise and opportunity.

Understanding "action research in the classroom" requires us to consider the elements and conditions that are essential. Johnson provided a succinct and explicit definition.

> Action research is deliberate, solution-oriented investigation that is group or personally owned and conducted. It is characterized by spiraling cycles of problem identification, systematic data collection, reflection, analysis, data-driven action taken, and finally, problem redefinition. The linking of the terms "action" and "research" highlights the essential features of this method; trying out ideas in practice as a means of increasing knowledge about/or improving curriculum, teaching, and learning. (Johnson, 1993, p. 1)

This definition encompasses the steps and conditions associated with action research. In this specific project that we undertook, we utilized this definition and these conditions to facilitate the inquiry processes to be employed by our candidates. We were anxious to consider the uses of action research as a change strategy for professional development among prospective teacher candidates. A concomitant condition was that this would be enhanced and improved through technological applications.

DESCRIBING THE PROCESS

Brigham Young University was fortunate to be provided a federally sponsored grant with the "Preparing Tomorrow's Teachers to Use Technology" Initiative. The PT3 grant encouraged and stimulated a variety of in service and professional development opportunities. A significant effort was made to have an impact on prospective teachers, realizing that they would carry with them these skills and knowledge into their classrooms.

This specific project had four components of inquiry:

1. Could undergraduate teacher education candidates conduct meaningful action research investigations?
2. Could undergraduate teacher education candidates utilize technology to facilitate and enhance this project?
3. Would the use of action research and technology improve the quality of teacher candidates' projects, presentations, and assignments?
4. Would these prospective teachers be more reflective and self-inquiring about their teaching and learning?

A select number of teacher candidates were participating in the secondary cohort program in the Department of Teacher Education. They were introduced and instructed in the process and value of conducting action research projects while completing their clinical field experience. Initially, this was seen as a burden and extraneous activity. However, as the assignment progressed, they became more convinced and committed to the endeavor. A video was shown entitled *On the Path.* This is an illustration of the Teacher-of-the-Year and his involvement of his elementary classroom in a project of studying a path that transected through their town. The path was viewed from a variety of points of view and concerns. The result was an engaging, productive, and educational activity. This problem-based learning experience modeled the kinds of inquiry, research, application, and reflection that we hoped to obtain.

An assignment was proposed and initiated with these secondary education cohort students. They were asked to consider their practices and activities within the classroom and school. In a real sense, they identified problems and questions that actually existed. The goals were to sharpen and improve their action research skills, technology applications, and organizational and presentation abilities. They were to value their own efforts through a problem-based, group-examined project. Identifying a meaningful and relevant concern, creating a project plan and strategy, conducting an intense study and examination, integrating a variety of skills and tasks, and carefully monitoring and adjusting for the effectiveness of the program maximized the effectiveness and efficiency of the teacher's and students' efforts. This was an investigation that exemplified "constructivism" at its best.

The first task was the identification of a concern, problem, or issue worthy of study and examination. This was generated from the cohort's own experience as teachers and as professional learners. The initiating stage encouraged self-analysis and reflection. As Windschitl would recommend, they were to:

1. create a problem-based learning experience,
2. identify significant inquiry activities,
3. promote dialogues with peers and teachers that encourage them to make sense of subject matter,
4. be exposed to multiple sources of information, and
5. find opportunities to demonstrate their understanding in diverse ways (Windschitl, 1999, p. 752).

A new image of the teacher was encouraged. "Teachers must try to arrive at a new vision of their role. This vision must include serving as a facilitator of learning who responds to students' needs with a flexible understanding of subject matter and a sensitivity to how the student is making sense of the world" (Windschitl, 1999, p. 753). This could not be taught by merely telling students about reflection, inquiry, problem identification, and research skills. For this reason, the students were provided opportunities for self-initiated, problem-based learning.

Literally, this project was intended to demonstrate to students that trivial and banal bits of knowledge are really inadequate in today's information technology age. They and their own students had to be more responsible and involved in their own learning. Marzano (1999) understood this when he talked about "deciding on 'essential knowledge.'" He said that the sheer amount of that which can be learned is overwhelming. Through action research, individuals can better determine that which is critically important, not only to themselves but to their profession. Technology is a vitally helpful tool and process that will encourage that inquiry and research.

This project was interesting in that we wished to identify the "effective use of technology" by teachers to help them do their work better. Indeed, there continues to be a dispute about the value and efficacy of technology in education. This is reflected in the questioning of what students in the schools actually learn by using technology.

> Just because children–particularly young ones–are performing tasks that look technologically sophisticated does not mean they are learning anything important. Moreover, the activity inevitably takes time and attention away from other types of learning. (Healy, 1998, p. 27)

Further, this discussion is somewhat disheartening to those who see the potential of technology. This has produced quite a dispute among educators. The entire learning process is being reassessed.

> How do they learn so much? Through experience, experimentation, and observation: tasting, smelling, hearing, touching. It is the real-life lessons–the climbing over and scooting under, putting one cup inside another, and chasing Cheerios around the kitchen floor–that teach a child how the world and his body work. Pushing a computer key to make an animated monkey dance does not have the same effect. (Kelly, 2000, p. 51)

This project was to take a more optimistic and productive analysis of technology and its impact on teaching and learning.

> Technology has become a sort of polestar for educators seeking ways to improve teaching and learning. They recognize that computers can motivate students to take more interest in and control of their learning. And despite the pains of hoeing the technology row–the costs, lack of teacher training, and lingering questions about technology's usefulness–each week brings fresh reports of how a school district or state is extending education's high-tech frontiers. (Allen, 2001, p. 2)

Technology was an integral part of this project. It was a way to facilitate and to improve the teaching and learning condition. Skills and understandings about technology were emphasized. Many of the students had completed the Intel "Teach to the Future Program," which encouraged the demonstration of planning, presentation, assessment, and classroom activities to enhance student learning.

A new kind of learning community and culture had to be creative. It was not intuitive or instinctive for teachers to think beyond their classroom. Rather, conventionally they were encouraged to avoid "wave-making" and risk-taking since this establishes a disquieting effect not only in their own classroom but the school. This project was to challenge these assumptions. In fact, all of the participants became convinced that working alone not only restricted meaningful change but turned teaching into a rather dull and ordinary endeavor. They realized that growth and improvement occurred in a collaborative environment with shared learning experiences, inquiring so that change could occur. "Autonomy equaled independence. Not so today. The problems and challenges in the workplaces of the 21st century are impossible to solve alone. That's one reason why teamwork is now the dominant mode of work nearly everywhere–except in education" (Wagner, 2001, p. 379). In our project, we sought "ownership rather than buy-in." As Wagner elaborated, "What is needed, in a word, is leadership that creates 'constructivist' adult learning–dialogue and critical inquiry" (Wagner, 2001, p. 380). Our students were advised that they would be spending a lot of time together, working on a shared and critically important issue for all, developing a sense of inquiry and thoughtfulness, and finding solutions of those problems that were meaningful to them. These students were assigned to study their teaching contexts and experiences. They were to identify an "essential question" about their practices, something that was perplexing and frustrating to them. Unsurprisingly, these students readily found things that warranted their study.

The cohort teachers proceeded in a scholarly and professional way. It was a pleasant surprise to find that none of them required direction or management. When presented with the task, they readily found there were things that they needed to be understood. They also recognized that no one was able or willing to study and solve their concerns but themselves. This proved to be an invaluable source of motivation and inspiration for the students. At the conclusion of the cohort student teaching experience, the cohort teams were asked to use technology to make a formal presentation for colleagues and, where appropriate, to other interested personnel. Motivated by their own commitment and involvement in their projects, we were anxious to consider the results. We wanted to contrast these projects and assignments with those traditionally conducted in a teacher education course. We wanted to ensure that technology was used both to acquire and organize the students' projects and also to present these in a more professional and scholarly way. Again, these were pleasant and convincing results that were identified.

CREATING A CLIMATE FOR STUDYING OUR PRACTICES

Change is something advocated by all but resisted by most. It inspires fear among the teaching world since this frequently means abandoning what has been comfortable and conventional. This project was asking prospective teachers to learn and to use technological hardware and innovative skills seldom seen in a regular classroom. It became apparent that Charles Dickens was right that "change begets change." Once introduced to the expectations and possibilities, these teachers expanded their willingness to incorporate and to use these newly acquired skills and tools.

RESULTS OF THE PROGRAM

At the conclusion of the cohorts' student teaching experience, we gathered in a final week of seminars and demonstrations. Since one of the initial goals was to encourage collaborative professional research and study, groups of students, usually two and three in number, were asked to make their presentations. They were told that they were to be considered a working study group within a faculty and making a presentation to a faculty in a school. These presentations were to demonstrate the use of technology, including the Internet, PowerPoint, and technical skills, such as movie clips and resource materials. Student teachers were told that they were to display reflection and thoughtfulness in their presentations.

> The action research process begins with serious reflection directed toward identifying a topic or topics worthy of a busy teacher's time. Considering the incredible demands on today's classroom teachers, no activity is worth doing unless it promises to make the central part of teacher's work more successful and satisfying. (Sagor, 2002, p. 4)

The presentations were made to the "student faculty members" with the intent of providing evidence and scholarly inquiry that they had initiated. Some of the topics included:

1. Curriculum Development: Impact and consequences of state and national curriculum standards upon instruction and classroom practices.
2. Standards and Accountability: Results of standards and publicly stated outcomes influencing school decisions and policies.
3. Tests and Evaluation: Student perceptions of tests and non-test measures relative to individual learning.
4. Discipline and Classroom Management: Teachers' recommendations and practices for effective discipline programs and classroom management strategies.
5. Moral Dimensions of Teaching: The moral tenets that direct and motivate teachers in the classroom, specifically John Goodlad's *Moral Dimensions of Teaching*.
6. Teaching for Character Education/Citizenship: Practices, programs, and research concerning the promotion of civic behavior and democratic principles.
7. Research and Effective Teaching: Research of "effective schools and teachers" and its relationship to their own classrooms and schools.
8. Planning to Teach: Evidence of teachers utilizing long-range planning, unit planning, and lesson planning as these relate to teacher practices.
9. Athletics and Co-Curricular Experiences: Student and teacher perceptions concerning the value and placement of extracurricular and co-curricular activities in the schools.

We were impressed with the depth and value of the projects undertaken by the students. They were readily motivated by the value and interest that these projects held for them. At the end of each presentation to the faculty, discussions, dialogue, and questions were initiated. The students had to respond and make recommendations relative to their projects. In some cases, suggestions were made to improve their research design, statistical analysis, and technology resources. This was done in a positive and supportive manner. When it was understood that all would have to participate and to share, they became learners and colleagues in the enterprise.

LESSONS LEARNED

We returned to the four underlying and initial assumptions that we made. First: *Could undergraduate, teacher education candidates conduct meaningful action research investigations?* In no sense were the students abandoned to their own devices. Regular "work sessions" were conducted. One of the teacher mentors is a recognized authority and leader in technology education. Additionally, she is a mathematics educator. Using these skills, she served the students well in improving their skills and knowledge concerning using technology, improving research and computational skills, and conducting meaningful inquiry strategies. The students developed and performed these well. Videotapes and evaluations were conducted to document and study the research skills of the students.

Second: *Could undergraduate teacher education candidates utilize technology to facilitate and enhance this project?* Too often, there has been a concern that teaching prospective teachers about technology is an exercise in skill mastery rather than technology application. An issue has been that technology would be a thing that real teachers did not use in professional ways. Technology should and could be used to do more than record keeping and completing peripheral tasks. This was one assignment that required a pragmatic utilization of the skills, knowledge, and dispositions associated with technology. The intent was to use technology as professional educators would in a school setting. Again, this was more than just learning some skills. It was an actual integration of technology into a realistic task and assignment.

Third: *Would the use of action research and technology improve the quality of teacher candidates' projects, presentations, and assignments?* One of introductory discussions with the students was dealing with "authentic learning" and "authentic assessments." The conversation generally evolved into the worthless and artificial tasks that they had done in other classes. We warned them that they too would be teachers and asking their students to complete tasks. The dialogue was about "wastebasket assignments" that are discarded in the wastebasket as students depart the classroom. Therefore, we wanted to find out if students felt ownership and responsibility for their projects. Did they own their own work? Did they sense accomplishment and professional contribution because of the task? Again, we were exceptionally pleased. They had identified their own problems. They had opportunities to study and to learn about them. They related them to their own experiences and classrooms. The students were motivated and responsive, reflective and thoughtful.

Unsurprisingly, some of the students felt that this was the most significant outcome from their cohort student teaching experience.

Most of these students had completed a traditional instructional technology course in their undergraduate preparation program. In that initial experience, the students were asked to demonstrate competence and mastery of certain technology skills and tasks. Even after taking this instructional technology course, the students noted a lingering concern. They felt that in this traditional computer class one element was missing. Although learning some basic skills and capabilities, they had not made a real connection to the needs of teachers in the classroom. Contrastingly, we had hoped in this cohort assignment that our students would generate real results. These would be authentic and genuine, not artificial or contrived. They would be useful to themselves and to practicing teachers. We did not want this to be merely an academic or technological activity. We had hoped for a critical connection to the actual role and assignment as a classroom teacher. We hoped that "real teacher problems" were to be solved and studied. Again, as we reviewed and assessed the cohort students' works, we were overwhelmingly pleased. Their action research and applications of technology had importance to themselves and to others. As indicated by the projects completed, the research conducted, the organization and presentation of information and results, and the functional uses of these efforts became evident. This was a major satisfaction with the project.

And fourth: *Would these prospective teachers be more reflective and self-inquiring about their teaching and learning?* Surveys and interviews were conducted with the students. Feedback forms provided us with some information. The cohorts found their experiences both affirming and insightful. For example, when one project dealt with discipline and classroom management, the students found that even experienced and veteran teachers were still concerned and apprehensive about management practices. They had believed that the "old pros" no longer had discipline and management concerns. Some of the teachers interviewed claimed that they did not receive sufficient support from and involvement of the administration. This was insightful to the neophyte teachers. They had previously assumed that teachers felt universal support from their administrators and staff. This was not evident from the cohort projects. Additionally, the cohort student teachers found that faculty members were divided on the value and importance of co-curricular activities, including school athletic programs. Several of the cohort student teachers were also serving as part-time coaches. Through their project, they became aware of the concern of many faculty members with the predominance and interference caused by these same programs. Using Internet resources, they found materials and demonstrations of effective practices that they could use and share with others.

The cohort student teachers saw reflectivity as a consequence of their inquiry. They acquired needful and beneficial skills and abilities. They mirrored what Barth advocated: "Reflection is precisely the capacity to distance oneself from the highly routinized, depleting, sometimes meaningless activities in which we are engaged, so that we can really see what's going on" (Barth, 2001, p. 65). The students readily acknowledged that they not only had learned things about teaching and schools but also about themselves. When considering the recommendations and characteristics identified as learning communities and teachers as researchers, they too noted substantial changes that had occurred:

- There was a focus for ambitious teaching and academic achievement.
- The students developed a keen attention to their students and their needs.
- They engaged in ongoing inquiry as a basis for continual improvement.
- They worked as team members who had been given more autonomy and authority for their own work.
- They identified greater opportunities to learn.
- There was an emphasis on teamwork.
- They identified the value of investment in continuous training.
- The students identified a "constancy of purpose."
- They noted that decision making was based on data collected by the working team (Darling-Hammond, 1997, pp. 150-151).

Reflection as a goal and outcome was fundamental to this enterprise. Information was obtained from the students to demonstrate this reflective component. Some of these feedback observations from the students included:

> Student 1: "I know that teaching is hard, but worth it. There are rewards, but sometimes they are slow in coming. I know my material and some methods."
> Student 2: "I have a moral obligation to help students have equal access to knowledge, which means equity–for example, there should be good ESL programs in place, and I can make adjustments in assessment for students with different backgrounds."
> Student 3: "We know they are eager, but will they also take the

easy way out if given the chance? They will rise to expectations."
Student 4: "I know I'm not perfect and need to keep learning. I know I want to be a teacher."

These and other statements were made to reflect the thoughtfulness and insightful inquiry of the cohort student teachers. This paralleled their endeavors to study their own practices and their own decisions.

Another lesson that was learned from this problem-solving, technology-facilitated, action-research project was the value of risk taking and professional development. Too often, teachers become complacent and satisfied, comfortable in what they are doing and what they are. By engaging these cohort student teachers to step out of traditional roles, they were required to becoming risk-taking learners. They learned a critical lesson that professional growth is inherent on the individual educator asking questions, seeking answers, finding ways to collect data, implementing change strategies, and continually sharing his/her experience. "Experimentation is risky. We rarely know in advance what will give us life and what will sap life away. But if we want to deepen out understanding of our own integrity, experiment we must–and then be willing to make choices as we view the experimental results" (Palmer, 1998, p. 16).

Another lesson learned was the substantial vision and perceptions that were developed by the cohort student teachers during this experience. First, they noted that schools were "data-rich" environments. Teachers could find data to solve their problems and enlighten their concerns. Second, they all commented that teaching and learning were dynamic and engaging. These were not passive events nor were the actors dull and boring. They became excited about the exciting places that we call school. Third, schools are places where self-examination and reflection of thoughtfulness and meaningfulness can and must occur. This made them see the culture and climate of the schools as a different place from what they had previously experienced. Fourth, they all acknowledged that there was much to be learned, both by teachers and students. Learning did not cease upon completion of the program and the obtaining of a degree. And fifth, new tools for learning and teaching were available, ready to be used, acknowledging that resources are available to facilitate that learning and teaching.

CONCLUSIONS

In conclusion, we were pleased with our experiences and results. We too were learners and yet, the cohort student teachers were the real learners. They learned both process and products. They were inquirers about their profession. They saw this enterprise as making a difference for themselves and for their profession. Action research and technology resources were valuable tools to these new teachers. Albert Einstein would have applauded the results: "He who can no longer pause to wonder and stand rapt in awe, is as good as dead; his eyes are closed" (Collected quotes from Albert Einstein, n.d.).

REFERENCES

Allen, R. (2001, Fall). Technology and learning. *Curriculum Update,* 1-3, 6-8.

Barth, S. (2001). *Learning by heart.* San Francisco: Jossey-Bass.

Bronowski, J. (1973). *The ascent of man.* Boston: Little, Brown and Company.

Cole, A. L., & Knowles, J. G. (2000). *Researching teaching: Exploring teacher development through reflexive inquiry.* Boston: Allyn & Bacon.

Collected quotes from Albert Einstein. (n.d.). Retrieved January 15, 2004, from http:rescomp.stanford.edu/~cheshire/EinsteinQuotes.html

Darling-Hammond, L. (1997). *The right to learn.* San Francisco: Jossey-Bass.

Fullan, M., & Hargreaves, A. (1996). *What's worth fighting for in your school.* New York: Teachers College Press.

Healy, J. M. (1998). *Failure to connect.* New York: Simon and Schuster.

Hunt, Jr., J. B., & Carroll, T. G. (2003). *No dream denied: A pledge to America's children: Summary report.* Washington, D.C.: National Commission on Teaching and America's Future.

Johnson, B. (1993). *Teacher as researcher.* Washington, D.C.: Clearinghouse on Teacher Education. (ERIC Document Reproduction Service No. ED 355205).

Kelly, K. (2000, September 25). False promise. *U.S. News and World Report, 129*(12), 48-55.

Marzano, R. J. (1999, April 22). Deciding on "essential knowledge." *Education Week, 18*(32), 68.

Palmer, P. J. (1998). *The courage to teach.* San Francisco: Jossey-Bass.

Sagor, R. (2002). *Guiding school improvement with action research.* Alexandria, Virginia: Association for Supervision and Curriculum Development.

Wagner, T. (2001). Leadership for learning. *Phi Delta Kappan, 82*(5), 378-383.

Windschitl, M. (1999). The challenges of sustaining a constructivist classroom culture. *Phi Delta Kappan, 80*(10), 751-755.

Wineburg, S., & Grossman, P. (1998). Creating a community of learners among high school teachers. *Phi Delta Kappan, 79*(5), 350-353.

Tina Taylor Dyches
Barbara A. Smith
Suraj Syal

Redesigning an Introduction to Special Education Course by Infusing Technology

SUMMARY. Online instruction is a growing method of delivering course content in higher education. However, little research has been conducted regarding the effectiveness of such instruction for pre-service teachers, in both general education and special education, who will teach students with disabilities. In this chapter we briefly review the literature regarding online instruction as it relates to pre-service special education.

TINA TAYLOR DYCHES is Associate Professor and Program Director for Special Education, Department of Counseling Psychology and Special Education, Brigham Young University, Provo, UT 84602 (E-mail: tina_dyches@byu.edu).
BARBARA A. SMITH is Assistant Clinical Professor of Special Education, Department of Teacher Education, Brigham Young University, Provo, UT 84602 (E-mail: bms5@email.byu.edu).
SURAJ SYAL is a Masters Candidate, Department of Counseling Psychology and Special Education, Brigham Young University, Provo, UT 84602 (E-mail: suajs@provo.k12.ut.us).

This course development project is funded through a PT3 grant through the Brigham Young University School of Education. The authors gratefully acknowledge the work of Betty Ashbaker, Gordon Gibb, James Young, and Lynn Wilder, their colleagues at Brigham Young University, for their extensive and ongoing contributions to this project.

[Haworth co-indexing entry note]: "Redesigning an Introduction to Special Education Course by Infusing Technology." Dyches, Tina Taylor, Barbara A. Smith, and Suraj Syal. Co-published simultaneously in *Computers in the Schools* (The Haworth Press, Inc.) Vol. 21, No. 1/2, 2004, pp. 59-72; and: *Integrating Information Technology into the Teacher Education Curriculum: Process and Products of Change* (ed: Nancy Wentworth, Rodney Earle, and Michael L. Connell) The Haworth Press, Inc., 2004, pp. 59-72. Single or multiple copies of this article are available for a fee from The Haworth Document Delivery Service [1-800-HAWORTH, 9:00 a.m. - 5:00 p.m. (EST). E-mail address: docdelivery@haworthpress.com].

Digital Object Identifier: 10.1300/J025v21n01_05

Then we describe our involvement with the Brigham Young University PT3 grant, our personal development in using technology in our courses, the development and refining of an Introduction to Special Education course, and contributions made by our students. Recommendations for future study and practice are provided. *[Article copies available for a fee from The Haworth Document Delivery Service: 1-800-HAWORTH. E-mail address: <docdelivery@haworthpress.com> Website: <http://www.HaworthPress.com> © 2004 by The Haworth Press, Inc. All rights reserved.]*

KEYWORDS. Special education, higher education, technology, online learning

INTRODUCTION

Most teacher education programs in the United States require pre-service teachers to take an Introduction to Special Education course. Such courses are often taught using traditional lecture formats. At Brigham Young University we have completely changed the way we teach our Introduction to Special Education course, from a face-to-face format to one which is now delivered primarily via electronic means. A PT3 grant provided necessary resources and instruction to enable our design team to redesign the course. Participation in this grant also provided our team with motivation to think differently about how we plan, deliver, and evaluate our instruction.

In this paper we review the literature regarding electronic learning in teacher education and describe the personal and course development processes that occurred while infusing technology into our Introduction to Special Education course.

REVIEW OF LITERATURE

Electronic learning or "e-learning" has been referred to as technology-mediated distance education, which includes online courses as well as two-way interactive television (Beattie, Spooner, Jordan, Algozzine, & Spooner, 2002). The Internet is a relatively new tool that has unprecedented potential for sharing information and expanding access to that information. According to the U.S. Department of Education (2001), 97% of full-time faculty and staff at two- and four-year institutions of higher education in the United States have access to the Internet, and 40% use Web sites to post course-related information. It has been noted that "technological applications to the delivery of university-level courses, like the Internet, are perhaps the most dynamic and pervasive breakthrough of information technology realized during this century" (Beattie et al., 2002, pp. 128-129).

The Internet is changing the delivery of instruction for many institutions of higher education. For example, the Office of Special Education Programs (OSEP) has produced 22 online modules for teacher education that have been adopted by over 160 universities (Meyen, Aust, Bui, & Isaacson, 2002). In 1998, approximately 710,000 students enrolled in at least one online course, and enrollment was predicted to reach 2.2 million by the year 2002 (Meyen et al., 2002).

As online courses become more prevalent in higher education, the implications for special education must be examined. According to the U.S. Department of Education (1995), there continues to be high attrition rates among those employed in special education. Further, shortages of qualified special educators throughout the United States are prevalent. Online courses reach wider audiences than traditional classes taught on campus and, thus, the enhanced potential in meeting teacher shortages is obvious, especially in areas where demand is high and the supply of skilled licensed teachers is low (Beattie et al., 2002).

Some may argue that, although online courses reach wider audiences, access to computers is still problematic. On the contrary, the 2000 United States Internet Council predicts that the number of users worldwide will pass the one billion mark by 2005 (Meyen et al., 2002). Furthermore, increasing the percentage of the American population familiar with computer technology and broadening access to information streaming via the Internet has become an important policy goal for governments at the local, state, and federal levels (Kastsinas & Moeck, 2002). "The rapid uptake of new technologies is occurring among most groups of Americans, regardless of income, education, race or ethnicity, location, age, or gender, suggesting that digital inclusion is a realizable goal" (Kastsinas & Moeck, 2002, p. 217). Although connectivity to all households is not a reality, rural community colleges are often the leading postsecondary institution for delivering online access (Kastsinas & Moeck, 2002).

Most of the existing research examining the effects of distance learning has not included special education. However, the research among the broader field is not conclusive regarding effectiveness of traditional face-to-face delivery compared with distance learning (Beattie et al.,

2002). Some research indicates that students, if given a choice, prefer to take a course "live" (Russell, 1997). Extensive research dating back to the 1920s indicates that "no matter how it is produced, how it is delivered, whether or not it is interactive, low-tech, or high-tech, students learn equally well with each technology and learn as well as their on-campus, face-to-face counterparts even though students would rather be on campus with the instructor if that were a real choice" (Russell, 1997, p. 6).

Live courses have many benefits to professors and students. First, professors can organize, monitor, and evaluate many activities that can only occur in person. Role plays, disability awareness activities, simulations, and personal experience listening and talking to individuals with disabilities are common activities in Introduction to Special Education courses. These activities are often used to help pre-service teachers develop tolerance, understanding, and sensitivity toward individuals with disabilities. It is not clear whether similar, or completely different activities delivered via the Internet would create the same levels of acceptance of persons with disabilities.

Further, live courses provide university students opportunities to practice basic methods that are effective in teaching students with disabilities. As Introduction to Special Education courses are often the only course required for elementary and early childhood majors regarding teaching students with disabilities, it is critical that they not only exit the class with heightened acceptance of students with disabilities, but also with a greater understanding of their legal responsibilities and rights, and a repertoire of basic teaching strategies for students with special needs.

Teaching in an Online Course

It can be argued that distance education courses tend to be typically a digitized version of the traditional instruction format. The literature on distance education concurs that instructors will not be successful at a distance by just doing what they have typically done in the traditional classroom. Poor teaching will be exacerbated in a distance education setting; meanwhile, if the instructor is good, the technology used to mediate the instruction is almost invisible (Beattie et al., 2002).

The literature suggests that most instructors are initially reluctant, but eventually willing to take initiative and begin to teach in such Web-based programs provided they are supported with appropriate training, time, and resources (Cerny & Heines, 2001; Cooper, 1999; Coppola &

Thomas, 2000; White, 2000). Time commitment for online teachers is much higher than traditional teaching because such courses typically take much longer to develop than traditional courses. Based on comments made by faculty, it is apparent that teaching online courses involves more instructional time than teaching campus-based classes (Sun, Bender, & Fore, 2003).

Students' Feelings About Receiving Online Instruction

Dr. Kubala from the University of Central Florida evaluated all of his students upon their completion of his online course (Kubala, 1998). All respondents said that the course met their learning needs and would recommend similar online courses to their friends. Ninety-four percent of the students said they felt adequately connected to the instructors and they received adequate attention as compared to traditional face-to-face classes. Eighty-one percent of the students said they preferred taking Web-based courses. Ninety percent of the students said they would like to try a combination of Web-based and traditional course formats. When students were asked what they liked most about their online courses, words like "flexibility" and "convenience" were at the head of the list (Kubala, 1998). Research shows that many higher education students respond favorably to courses delivered via distance education and believe that this option offers learning opportunities similar to traditional classes (Sun et al., 2003).

The results of existing studies suggest that the overall decision to implement Web-based training for teachers of students with disabilities may well rest on other relevant data such as faculty and/or student satisfaction, an increase in the demand for courses, increased time/schedule flexibility due to an increase in enrollment of graduate students or teachers seeking special education certification and who work full-time, or overall program evaluations (Sun et al., 2003). In short, "ultimately, students will be the judges of the effectiveness of distance education delivery" (Sun et al., 2003, p. 92).

Academic Outcomes for Those Who Participate in Traditional and Distance Education Courses

Several studies in higher education have compared academic outcomes between Web-based courses and traditional courses and results indicate that student learning in Web-based courses is not different from learning in comparable on-campus courses (Sun et al., 2003).

Schulman and Sims (1999) completed a test-retest research study designed to measure the learning of students in online and traditional classes. There was no significant difference in the average post-test scores for the two groups. "End-of-course student evaluations (e.g., overall mean and component evaluations, course, instructor, organization, teaching, and communication) suggested no differences for overall course means" (Beattie et al., 2002, p. 125). Research demonstrates evidence of comparable learning between online students and traditional class students (Schulman & Sims, 1999; Coppola & Thomas, 2000; Ryan, 2000; Cooper, 2001).

In comparing the same special education course offered by the same instructor, one taught on campus and the other via distance education, findings revealed there were no differences in student ratings in the area of course evaluation items, instructor evaluation items, and general evaluation items, and that the result of "no difference" was favorable (Beattie et al., 2002). In this study, two positive aspects of providing an online course included: Enrollment in the course increased fourfold with students' perceiving they received key aspects of instruction; and the instructor had the ability and flexibility to make pedagogical changes in order to reach the students at the remote sites without hindering student learning (Beattie et al., 2002).

The current project was an ongoing attempt to redesign an Introduction to Special Education course that was previously taught using a traditional lecture format. These revisions entailed a complete overhaul of the course, with an emphasis on technologically delivered instruction while retaining elements of personalization that students enjoy in such a class.

INVOLVEMENT WITH THE PT3 GRANT

Our faculty design team was created because we had a need that was being unmet; that is, the Introduction to Special Education course was not being delivered efficiently or effectively. Dr. Dyches had previously been involved in the PT3 grant by taking the recommended Instructional Psychology and Technology course, and was approached by Dr. Nancy Wentworth to assemble a design team. Selected team members included Barbara Smith, who, on many occasions, expressed an interest in using technology in her classes, and Suraj Syal, at that time a technology specialist in one of our partnership school districts.

We attended a summer institute, a three-day workshop in the McKay School of Education, where we learned basic skills to develop a WebQuest for our course. As we viewed examples from other professionals, we developed guiding questions and brainstormed to find appropriate Web sites for our WebQuest. The format of this workshop allowed us to not only learn basic skills, but to actually create a WebQuest. We also received feedback from other teams regarding how it could be improved, and following the workshop, we met frequently to implement these suggestions. Later, we would develop three more WebQuests for inclusion in our course.

Our technological skills were enhanced further with our participation in monthly Brown Bag meetings, which were offered through the PT3 grant. We were able to network with other professors in the School of Education and to learn how we could share resources. We also learned many skills, including how to use Blackboard more effectively, how to use various software programs, and how we could use handheld computers in our classes.

When handheld computers became available for use in our course, we decided to infuse this to assist student learning. Thirty-five IPAQ handheld computers and keyboards were available for pre-service teachers to check out and use for the term. They received two hours of training and then were free to set up a partnership with their personal or lab computer. Later, as each pre-service teacher tutored children with disabilities in the public schools, they kept a learning log on their IPAQs. Each time the class met, the students turned in their logs and other assignments by beaming it to the professor. Feedback regarding the use of these handheld computers was positive.

Two members of our design team were able to present a summary of our work at the 14th Annual Society for Information Technology in Teacher Education Conference in Albuquerque, New Mexico. We networked with other professionals in special education and general education and learned many other practical ways to use technology in our program.

PERSONAL DEVELOPMENT IN USING TECHNOLOGY

All three of us on our design team were reasonably comfortable with using technology, but had not previously worked on a team to substantially impact the delivery of a university course. Working on a team decreased the amount of work one person might have to accomplish in revising our course, and it allowed us to synergistically create learning activities that would effectively meet course objectives using technology.

Our involvement with the PT3 grant encouraged us to take an alternative view of the way we taught our course. Instead of adding to the class a few assignments that use technology, we redesigned the course to be dependent on technology.

Further, as we continued to receive instruction through the PT3 grant, we became more aware of software and hardware that was available to us at our university, and we began to access those resources. Such networking has been a great benefit to our team and to the development of our course.

COURSE DEVELOPMENT

Our Introduction to Special Education course, "Counseling Psychology and Special Education 400: Exceptional Students: Principles of Collaboration," is required for all elementary, special, and early childhood education majors at Brigham Young University. It may soon be required for all secondary education majors as well, increasing the number of students enrolled annually from approximately 500 to over 1,000.

This course had been taught for decades by individual professors teaching one or two sections using a traditional format, where the professor gave a lecture regarding a "disability of the week," and students read chapters from a textbook. Technological enhancements to the class were determined by individual professors and, if utilized, were limited to viewing of video clips of students with disabilities.

Various changes in the teacher education programs at BYU necessitated changes in the way CPSE 400 was delivered. Many options were considered, including using the same lecture format to teach the course to only a few sections per semester with large class sizes (approximately 100 students per class). However, the option agreed upon by the professors who taught this course was to deliver the course using our own text via the Internet, while still retaining several sections taught by several professors.

Most of the professors (five of the six) in the department wrote the text and obtained assistance from BYU's Center for Instructional Design in developing interactive mastery checks, online quizzes and exams, and graphics for the text. This package was then available via Blackboard, an Internet-based course management program, as an html document, and through Perception, an assessment management tool. Some professors initially used other features of Blackboard, such as course information, course documents, announcements, gradebook, and e-mail. As the professors gained confidence in their use of Blackboard, they began to use other features, such as external links, digital drop box, discussion board, and assessment manager.

Over the years the format for course delivery progressed from face-to-face, to Internet only, then to a hybrid of the two formats. The current course configuration is a hybrid which requires approximately ten 50-minute class sessions that are spent engaging in typical face-to-face activities (e.g., group discussion, viewing videotapes, role-playing, solving case studies). The online portion of the class requires students to (a) complete the readings and mastery checks online, (b) complete the quizzes and exams online, (c) engage in electronic discussions with classmates, (d) gain supplementary information by visiting recommended or self-selected external Web sites, and (e) submit a portfolio of their work to the professor via digital drop box. All of these activities are available through Blackboard and most of its features are used by the professors.

As we progressed in our ability to infuse technology into this course, we developed additional assignments for this class. A few of these will be discussed.

First, four of the lessons now have a WebQuest, which is an exploratory, Web-based, interactive method of learning that is student-directed. Pre-service teachers are presented with a problem to solve or a question to answer, and are required to access resources available on the Internet to solve the problem. They are then required to use technology to convey to their peers the information they learned. For example, in the first WebQuest that deals with using person-first language, pre-service teachers are guided through various Web-based activities, and then are required to create a PowerPoint presentation that they would use in a faculty meeting to teach other educators about how labels can affect students with disabilities.

Another technological component is the integration of videotaped interviews and footage of teachers using effective practices. Approximately 20 experts in the field of special education have been interviewed and these tapes are currently being digitized for use in the course. They will be available as Quicktime files for students to access while they are engaged in the online lessons. Footage of teachers using effective practices that have been discussed in the text or by the videotaped experts will also be available for students to view as part of the course. This will give students a much broader perspective of the salient issues in special education than they would have previously been given had they just read a text or listened to the lectures of one professor.

Because we have eliminated the use of a textbook in this course, we have required the students to engage in self-directed learning activities via the Internet. However, some students prefer having a paper copy of the text for current and future access. These students are able to print off each page of the online text, or they can purchase a packet from the bookstore that contains the text and lesson activities.

Historically, students in this class have been required to demonstrate their competency through three unit exams. However, recognizing that other assignments might allow students to demonstrate their knowledge and skills more effectively, the professors have allowed the students alternatives to taking these exams. One of these alternatives includes completing a CD-ROM program, "What's Best for Matthew?" (Egan, Dyches, Young, Ingram, Gibb, & Allred, 2000) to learn about the Individualized Education Program process for students with disabilities. Another alternative is to view a videotape regarding how to teach students with learning disabilities, then to write a report about effective strategies.

Finally, students in this course are part of a pilot program that investigates the use of handheld computers in the university classroom. As part of their requirement to serve a child with disabilities for 12 hours throughout the semester, these pre-service teachers are required to complete a learning log to account for their time with the student. They have been given an IPAQ handheld computer and keyboard, where they complete their learning log while in the public school, and beam their logs to the professor on a weekly basis, rather than at the end of their experience. By doing so, the professor is able to help the pre-service teachers with any pressing issues while they are still in the classroom.

With the reinstatement of a major in special education at BYU, another course configuration has been added as a requirement for those intending to earn their license in special education. These students are required to take the "live" version of the course for two 50-minute periods per week throughout the semester. At least one of these sections is taught in the afternoon for those teachers who are returning to the university to obtain their special education license. Although the students in the live classes have many face-to-face learning activities, the hybrid nature of the course remains. They engage in the same electronic activities as those who are not majoring in special education, yet have the additional time needed in the class in order to serve specifically as future special educators.

Also, CPSE 400 is still offered via independent study, and many students from BYU as well as other universities throughout the nation choose to complete the course completely online. Students taking the course via this configuration are allowed up to one year to complete their coursework. One of our professors in the department manages this independent study course as an addition to his regular teaching load.

Thus, three configurations of CPSE 400 are currently in existence. We believe this offers students the flexibility to choose the section that most closely aligns with their individual learning styles. As a result, this course allows students individual choice in their learning activities, including (a) how to take the course (e.g., independent study, hybrid, or live), (b) how to access the text (e.g., online or printed), (c) how to take the exams (e.g., multiple-choice exam, video review, CD-ROM activities), (d) when to take the course (e.g., day or evening sections and online only), and (e) the length of time to complete the course (e.g., from a few weeks to one year).

This is a work-in-progress project that is being refined to better meet the needs of school districts in our area, the faculty who teach this course, and the pre-service teachers who take this course. Current and future development of the course will require continued teamwork in analyzing the effectiveness of this course.

CONTRIBUTIONS MADE BY OUR STUDENTS

The pre-service teachers who have taken this class throughout the last few years have provided solicited and unsolicited critiques of CPSE 400. Although some of their comments may have been difficult to accept (e.g., on-campus students not liking the online-only version of the course), they pushed us to make important changes in the way we delivered the course. As a result, CPSE 400 is now a course that is enjoyed by students and professors alike.

Presently many of the pre-service teachers' assignments involve technological components (e.g., accessing Web sites and electronic discussions, submitting assignments electronically). One particularly useful assignment is for them to explore a useful Web site that deals with a specific disability, then to share the Web site address along with a description of what is included on the site, and what is particularly helpful to them as pre-service teachers. They post these on our course discussion board for all students to access. Many of these Web sites will be included as permanent external links for the course, and were not previously accessed or used by the professors. Having a list of Web sites that are selected by general educators will be important to future pre-service teachers, as those that are selected by professors of special education may be too technical for a broader audience.

With the inclusion of WebQuests, our students will be adding to the information base of their peers as they share their work with their peers and professors. We anticipate that in the future we will have our pre-service teachers use technology more directly with the students with disabilities and report on its effectiveness.

RECOMMENDATION FOR STUDY AND PRACTICE

We have gathered data from the various phases of development of this course (e.g., live, online, hybrid). These data include quiz scores, exam scores, portfolio scores, and scores on an attitude toward students with disabilities scale. We will analyze these data to determine which method of delivering this course is most effective and efficient in preparing pre-service teachers to teach students with disabilities in their classrooms.

Other special education professors in higher education may consider delivering course content via electronic means when they do not have the resources to provide several sections of the same course, want to engage students in meaningful learning experiences, and enhance students' technological attitudes and skills. Because there is a paucity of research in this area, it is recommended that such work be systematically documented and its effectiveness researched.

CONCLUSION

This Introduction to Special Education course has evolved from a lecture-based course, to strictly online, and finally to a hybrid delivery format. Currently all three configurations are offered, yet are completely different from their original format. This is due to the infusion of technology throughout the course. Had the course remained in its traditional "face-to-face" format, it is unlikely the technological components would have been developed, refined, and utilized. The students appear to be more comfortable with this course, likely because they are given the opportunity to choose how they will take it. As more technological elements are infused into the course, further evaluations and refinements will take place, providing pre-service teachers with the technological skills necessary to be successful in today's classrooms.

REFERENCES

Beattie, J., Spooner, F., Jordan, L., Algozzine, B., & Spooner, M. (2002). Evaluating instruction in distance learning classes. *Teacher Education and Special Education, 25*(2), 124-132.

Cerny, M., & Heines, J. (2001). Evaluating distance education across twelve time zones. *T. H. E. Journal Online: Technological Horizons in Education, 28*(7). Retrieved December 3, 2003, from http://www.thejournal.com/magazine/vault/A3296.cfm

Cooper, L. (1999). Anatomy of an online course. *T. H. E. Journal Online: Technological Horizons in Education, 26*(7). Retrieved December 3, 2003, from http://www.thejournal.com/magazine/vault/A2071.cfm

Cooper, L. (2001). Online and traditional computer applications class. *T. H. E. Journal Online: Technological Horizons in Education, 28*(8). Retrieved December 3, 2003, from http://www.thejournal.com/magazine/vault/A3387.cfm

Coppola, J., & Thomas, B. (2000). A model for e-classroom design: Beyond "chalk and talk." *T. H. E. Journal Online: Technological Horizons in Education, 27*(6). Retrieved December 3, 2003, from http://www.thejournal.com/magazine/vault/A2594.cfm

Egan, M. W., Dyches, T. T., Young, J. R., Ingram, C. F., Gibb, G. S., & Allred, K. W. (2000). *What's best for Matthew?* (Version 2). Needham Heights, MA: Allyn & Bacon.

Kastsinas, S. G., & Moeck, P. (2002). The digital divide and rural community colleges: Problems and prospects. *Community College Journal of Research and Practice, 26,* 207-224.

Kubala, T. (1988). Assessing students needs: Teaching on the Internet. *T. H. E. Journal Online: Technological Horizons in Education, 25*(8). Retrieved December 3, 2003, from http://www.thejournal.com/magazine/vault/A2026B.cfm

Meyen, E. L., Aust, R. J., Bui, Y. N., & Isaacson, R. (2002). Assessing and monitoring student progress in an e-learning personal preparation environment. *Teacher Education and Special Education, 25*(2), 187-198.

Russell, T. L. (1997). Explaining, exploring, understanding the no significant difference phenomenon. *Adult Assessment Forum. 7*(4), 6-9.

Ryan, R. (2000). Student assessment comparison of lecture and online construction equipment and methods classes. *T. H. E. Journal Online: Technological Horizons in Education, 27*(6). Retrieved December 3, 2003, from http://www.thejournal.com/magazine/vault/A2596.cfm

Schulman, A., & Sims, R. (1999). Learning in an on-line format versus an in-class format: An experimental study. *T. H. E. Journal Online: Technological Horizons in Education Journal.* Retrieved December 3, 2003, from http://www.thejournal.com/magazine/vault/A2090B.cfm

Sun, L., Bender, W. N., & Fore III, C. (2003). Web-based certification courses: The future of teacher preparation in special education? *Teacher Education and Special Education*, 26(2), 87-97.

U.S. Department of Education. (1995). *Seventeenth annual report to congress on the implementation of the Individuals with Disabilities Education Act.* Washington, DC: Author.

U.S. Department of Education. National Center for Educational Statistics. (2001). *The condition of education 2001.* Washington, DC: U.S. Government Printing Office.

White, C. (2000). Students and faculty respond to online distance courses at Grant Macewan Community College. *T. H. E. Journal Online: Technological Horizons in Education*, 27(9), Retrieved December 3, 2003, from http://www.thejournal.com/magazine/vault/A2814.cfm

Eula Monroe
Marvin Tolman

Using Technology in Teacher Preparation: Two Mature Teacher Educators Negotiate the Steep Learning Curve

SUMMARY. This paper chronicles the ventures of two mature faculty members who continue to negotiate their own steep learning curves in helping teacher education students use current technology. It describes the scaffolding provided within the university setting for the faculty members' growth. Included are elements supported by a PT3 grant that have enabled them to develop the vision, skills, attitudes, and courage necessary to stay the course willingly and without duress. Benefits to their students as well as to themselves are discussed, along with ongoing challenges to continued growth. *[Article copies available for a fee from The Haworth Document Delivery Service: 1-800-HAWORTH. E-mail address: <docdelivery@haworthpress.com> Website: <http://www.HaworthPress.com> © 2004 by The Haworth Press, Inc. All rights reserved.]*

EULA MONROE is Professor, Department of Teacher Education, Brigham Young University, Provo, UT 84602 (E-mail: eula_monroe@byu.edu).
MARVIN TOLMAN is Professor, Department of Teacher Education, Brigham Young University, Provo, UT 84602 (E-mail: marv_tolman@byu.edu).

[Haworth co-indexing entry note]: "Using Technology in Teacher Preparation: Two Mature Teacher Educators Negotiate the Steep Learning Curve." Monroe, Eula, and Marvin Tolman. Co-published simultaneously in *Computers in the Schools* (The Haworth Press, Inc.) Vol. 21, No. 1/2, 2004, pp. 73-84; and: *Integrating Information Technology into the Teacher Education Curriculum: Process and Products of Change* (ed: Nancy Wentworth, Rodney Earle, and Michael L. Connell) The Haworth Press, Inc., 2004, pp. 73-84. Single or multiple copies of this article are available for a fee from The Haworth Document Delivery Service [1-800-HAWORTH, 9:00 a.m. - 5:00 p.m. (EST). E-mail address: docdelivery@haworthpress.com].

KEYWORDS. Computers, staff development, learning curve, mature educators, technology, higher education

In 1908, psychologists Yerkes and Dotson reported a pattern of behavior that has been generalized over the past century to indicate the following: The higher the expectation for learning, the higher the performance–to a point. If the learner reaches a point at which the learning curve becomes too steep, then learning diminishes or disappears (see Figure 1).

> In the first part of the curve, stress [expectation] actually improves our efficiency. But past a certain point, the reverse occurs: ongoing stress impairs our effectiveness. In fact, working longer or harder beyond that point is not only unproductive, it's counter-productive. We might even call this the law of diminishing returns. (Posen, n.d.)

The delicate balance between expectation and achievement must be respected if optimal growth is to be achieved with any learner, especially mature university faculty (e.g., Farmer, 1993; Faseyitan & Hirschbuhl, 1992).

The authors of this paper, who are the "mature teacher educators" referred to in the title, were well into adulthood when scientific technology enabled Neil Armstrong to walk on the moon; it was several years later that the handheld calculator became inexpensive enough for com-

FIGURE 1

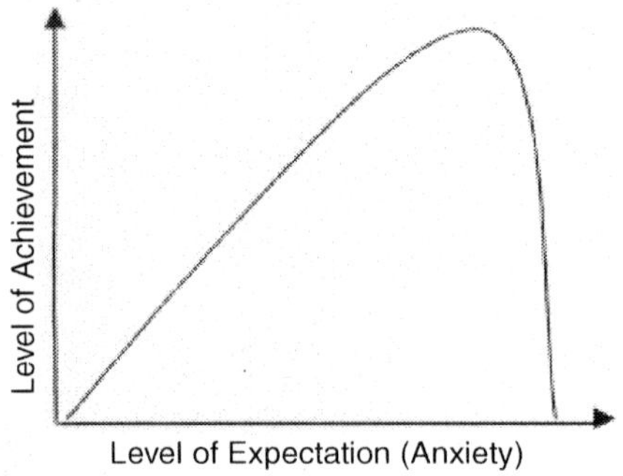

mon use. For even the most confident and venturesome senior faculty, the expectation to embrace changes in teaching and learning made possible by rapid technological advances can be intimidating. Among less willing learners, some may "dig in their heels," resisting change and using their positions of power that accompany rank and status to undermine the efforts of those who wish to nudge colleges of education into the 21st century technologically.

One might think that pre-service teachers who have grown up in an environment where the widespread use of computers and calculators is commonplace would have little difficulty accepting and using technology in their methods classes. However, for many elementary majors, courses that rely heavily on the Web, or even those that require frequent use of calculators or e-mail, can be intimidating. The mandate for teacher education is clear: Pre-service teachers must be prepared to help their students use technology appropriately. Regardless of the challenges posed, teacher educators must model, use, and teach the use of technology in their classes.

This paper chronicles the ventures of two mature teacher educators, one in elementary science education and the other in elementary mathematics education, who continue to negotiate their own steep learning curves in helping pre-service teachers learn to use current technology. It describes the scaffolding provided for their growth and includes elements supported by a PT3 grant that (a) have served as a catalyst in their development of the necessary vision, attitudes, and skills; and (b) have provided the encouragement for them to stay the course willingly and without duress. To their surprise, they have also had opportunities to provide leadership, helping to chart the course not only for their students but for some of their colleagues as well.

OUR PERSONAL TECHNO-AUTOBIOGRAPHIES

The Science Educator (Marvin Tolman)

I grew up in a small farming community in southeastern Idaho. Tractors were in, but local folks still used a lot of horse-drawn farming equipment. I was less than two years old when Pearl Harbor was bombed; my clearest memories of World War II are of sugar rations and the scarcity of sweets.

The first telephone in my memory was a wooden box with a crank on the side, and our first family car was started with a crank in front. I was

12 years old when the first TV set came to town, but in our home TV remained out of the question. Many Americans scoffed at Albert Einstein when he suggested that he could help the United States put a man on the moon. Perhaps to the surprise of these same Americans, Russia succeeded in making Sputnik the first man-made satellite to circle the planet Earth. In 1969 I joined the rest of the world in front of the TV with great anticipation as Neil Armstrong descended the ladder of the landing module and placed his foot on lunar soil, uttering these immortal words: "That's one small step for man, one giant leap for mankind."

My first personal use of a computer was using punch cards for an assignment in a statistics class in 1972. The combination of monitor and keyboard, which allows the user to interact with the computer, was unheard of. In 1974 I purchased my first calculator. I needed the square root function, and I found a calculator on sale for $100. It had no memory, but it could add, subtract, multiply, divide, and compute square root. That was all I needed, and it was all I could afford.

After I joined the Brigham Young University Elementary Education faculty in 1975, the next major computer event in my life came in 1981. I was aware that desk-model computers were on the market, but they had not yet invaded my life. While visiting student teachers in an elementary school, I saw two Commodore Pets being used by third-grade students. I quickly concluded that this technology was coming to the schools and I might as well accept the inevitable and join in. I immediately signed up for two programming courses (BASIC and Pascal), and I entered a technological whirlwind. Within three years I was teaching a computer literacy class for education majors (K-12) in the College of Education; I was also one of five authors working on a computer literacy textbook (first edition published in 1986 by Prentice Hall). One of the topics of the course was programming, using Logo, and we were so excited to be able to program the computer to draw images on the screen with "turtle graphics." By 1987 the computer literacy course had moved to the computer lab, with class instruction time greatly reduced, and I was no longer involved with the course.

During the intervening years, I have used the computer extensively in my work. Word processing, spreadsheets, e-mail, and the Internet have greatly enhanced my efficiency in my work. However, my expertise in using the computer has grown with an occasional pop of a firecracker within the mushroom cloud of exploding computer technology.

I have heard it said that children in recent history have been born with a digital gene. My experience supports that notion. Computer technology seems to run in the blood of the younger generation, while I struggle for each new skill that I try to learn. I consider myself very fortunate, however, to work at a university that places high value on the implementation of new technology and provides support in the acquisition of both software and hardware, along with ample opportunities for staff development in their use. Technical help is always near at hand when anything goes wrong with either the technology or the user's ability to make it work. A PT3 grant, managed by skilled faculty who kindly encouraged my progress, had an enormous impact on my growth as a user of technology.

The Mathematics Educator (Eula Monroe)

Born in a remote farming community in north Todd County, Kentucky, just prior to World War II, I grew up without feeling the direct impact of many of the technological advances that were common in more urban areas. I well remember our first radio. One fall day in 1945, when my older brother and sister and I returned home from the one-room country school we attended, we heard the miracle of voices emerging from under the bedsheet where my mother had hidden this technological marvel to surprise us. I studied by coal-oil lamp until I was well into high school, and we got both our first car and first television in 1957, during my senior year. Our first telephone came seven years later, in 1964, and the telephone company assigned us to a party line with several other families who lived up and down the highway. In those days, courteous phone use required serious attention; one had to remember when the phone rang last and allow ample time before picking up so as not to interrupt a conversation between two neighbors.

The more casual tempo of the '50s in regard to many aspects of life, including technology, was abruptly terminated by Russia's launching of Sputnik on October 4, 1957. Life was never to be the same again. The space race was on, with the scientific superiority of Russia, and Communism as well (according to the Russians), incontrovertibly demonstrated. Not quite 12 years later, on my 29th birthday, I was returning home from church when I heard the news flash that man had landed on the moon! "Impossible!" was the sentiment of many of my friends and neighbors in the rural area where I lived, but it was true. The United States had forged ahead in the space race with Russia, and there was no turning back.

The pace of technological change in my everyday life accelerated. When I entered my doctoral program in the summer of 1978, I was able to buy a four-function calculator with memory. All this for only $15.95!

I was told that the level of technology I held in my hand would have cost more than $100 not more than two years past. During my first doctoral-level statistics class, I was informed that I had the opportunity to learn twice as much because of the support this little calculator gave me.

My doctoral program was not without keypunching and verifying, sending little cards with square holes signifying the presence of descriptive data through a large computer. Other, more sophisticated, analyses were completed by hand with the help of calculators that had additional functions and more memory. I did my share of learning programming in BASIC (two courses), although I never figured out what use it was to me. In addition, I took courses to learn advancing technology; these I found more immediately useful.

During the early '80s, with the advent of the Apple 2e, I carted around one or more of these computers in the trunk of my car to various school sites, sharing this innovation with classroom teachers and other school personnel. I also worked with pre-service and in-service teachers to help them learn to use Logo as well as mathematics practice programs available from several large suppliers. I avoided word processing at first; typing had been the hardest course for me in high school, and I was slow to recognize the potential that the computer offered. I bought a Tandy, but it stayed in the box for almost a year because of my aversion to typing. Once converted to word processing, however, I acquired an available version of a laptop (a Tandy, much bigger and heavier than my current PowerBook G4, but portable) and took it through airports to conferences and on vacation–wherever I went.

The '90s multiplied my uses of the computer, and another milestone in technology occurred: The Internet became available, and, with it, e-mail. Some say that these developments are both a blessing and a curse, and I agree, for reasons the reader probably finds obvious. During the '90s I also became much more comfortable with my ability to help pre-service and in-service teachers use computers and related technology.

Even though I was called on to be more or less at the "cutting edge" in the use of technology in teacher education all these years, I experienced a steep learning curve with every new opportunity to learn anything that resembled a technological application. Technology use was not natural to me, although I was a willing learner if not put into potentially embarrassing situations. The connections I seemed to make more readily in other aspects of learning did not come easily in this domain. I do not know the source of this problem, but I hypothesize that I found it more difficult because I was such a latecomer to technology use.

Although my early years were admittedly more technologically aus-
tere than for most teacher educators, I currently have many colleagues
of varying age levels who also did not grow up using a high level of
technology. The use of a technology podium in a classroom or the construction of a Web site can still be a potential source of intimidation for
some. As I would expect, the learning curve remains steep for many of
us. Surprisingly, however, the case is similar for a large proportion of
our elementary education majors. Many students I encounter in the elementary schools are more technologically confident and proficient than
some of the pre-service and in-service elementary teachers with whom I
work.

UNIVERSITY AND PT3 SUPPORT

Nevertheless, we are making strides technologically, and we have
ample support to do so. Free tuition is available for any University
course faculty members wish to take, whether for credit or audit. Faculty can choose from a wide variety of University-sponsored workshops
on everything from using the Web or accessing library resources to using specific applications for which there is an interest and need. And,
when one has a technology-related question or problem, expert assistance is available within minutes or hours.

In addition to the University computer support network, a PT3 grant
greatly enhanced faculty technology development. As a part of this
grant, Apple Computer and other corporations, the Utah State Office of
Education, our School of Education, and personnel from departments
across the University provided specialists to conduct workshops to enhance our skills and understanding. Local school district specialists
joined us for some of our sessions, to share what they are doing to implement the available technology in their districts and to learn with us.
We learned to design Web pages, use BlackBoard, make iMovies from
digital photographs we took, adopt a tech podium as a regular part of our
teaching lives, and create WebQuests for our students. Even though
funding from the grant has ended, the list of opportunities goes on,
seemingly limited only by our time and energy to take advantage of
them.

These orientation and development efforts have been helpful to all
participants, but the rate of faculty progress in implementing the new
technology has varied greatly. Those who grew into it earlier in their
lives seem to have an advantage over those of us who remember when

copy machines rewarded the user with purple ink stains, and corrections were made with erasers that wore holes in originals. Yet there has been a spirit of collaboration, support, and progress among the faculty who have chosen to participate in technology-related activities, regardless of the level of development of the individual faculty member.

An anchor to collaboration in PT3 grant activities was the design team structure. We as faculty chose to be on various design teams according to academic discipline(s) or job-alike tasks, with the results being beneficial to each person involved. Some design team projects were targeted at improving our own skills in technology use; others were opportunities to develop products to be implemented in classes (e.g., technology-based lessons). We shared our products with one another in "brown bag" sessions, and more widely through presentations at regional and national conferences.

With support from the PT3 grant and the University to attend national and international conferences, we have learned from users of educational technology far and wide. It is during presentations and interactions at these conferences that we have experienced our major "aha" insights–moments when we have caught glimpses of the potential of technology as a transforming influence in our teacher preparation program. We have returned to BYU after each conference more committed than ever to help our students enter the schools prepared for the roles they are expected to assume as technologically capable classroom teachers.

STAYING THE COURSE–BENEFITS AND BARRIERS

We find three major categories of benefits from our willingness to negotiate steep learning curves for using current technology: (a) our increased fluency and flexibility with technology, (b) transformations in our methods courses as a result of technology use, and (c) increased use of technology by the pre-service and in-service teachers who take our courses. These benefits, along with barriers, are discussed in this section.

Increased Fluency and Flexibility with Technology

We are becoming more fluent and flexible in the use of technology in our day-to-day roles as professors of teacher education. We rejoice in pleasant surprises in already-familiar applications, and we learn new applications when we have projects that dictate the need. Our utilization has increased both in range and depth. We have become more self-sufficient when we encounter a problem but also more confident in framing our questions and stating our needs, knowing that help is as close as a neighbor down the hall or simply a phone call away. The opportunities we have for sharing our newfound "expertise" with other, often younger, colleagues who are struggling with similar problems are both surprising and validating.

Transformations in Our Methods Courses

We are experiencing the transformation that technology brings to our methods courses. Although we are far from having "arrived" (we suspect there is no such thing, and, if there is such a thing, it is a long way away for both of us!), we have witnessed the power of using Black-Board and of implementing a performance task that integrates mathematics and science through the use of the Internet, digital cameras, and spreadsheeting (http://msed.byu.edu/pt3/tree.html). We stand to the side as our students work on WebQuests we have created, and we delight in the technology tasks that many of our students undertake on their own initiative when they have choices in how to complete course assignments. We model the use of technology in our classes and give both in-class and out-of-class assignments that require the use of technology. (See Appendix for two examples of out-of-class assignments.)

Increased Use of Technology by Our Students

We are working diligently to help both pre-service and in-service teachers with whom we work learn to use current technology effectively with the children they serve. We require pre-service teachers to use technology in their field placements, and we rejoice when they connect with their elementary school students in mathematics and science through the use of technology. We emphasize the exploration and development of age- and content-appropriate tasks for elementary school students. When on occasion a methods student tells us that his or her cooperating teacher in the field "won't allow me to do a lesson in mathematics (or science) using technology," we look more deeply to find the source of the problem. Could it be that computers are not readily available, or that the student does not feel comfortable planning a lesson integrating the use of technology? Perhaps this student is exhibiting technology-avoidance behaviors, which emerge sporadically among our students.

We view the comfort level of our undergraduate students in the use of technology as mixed. Student access to technology on campus is readily available, and each student has taken a required course in the use of technology prior to our methods classes. However, based on student responses to in-class and out-of-class assignments involving technology, we hypothesize that, on a comfort-in-use scale, clumps of students would polarize at either end. Attaching a file to an e-mail message creates a challenge for some methods students, while developing Web pages and electronic newsletters appears to be almost second nature to others. In a small pilot study of two groups of pre-service teachers who had completed our courses, we found that respondents used e-mail, word processing, and a Web browser almost daily, but the use of applications such as spreadsheets, course message boards, streaming audio and video, and drawing and painting programs was rare. And, although both of us introduce and use the *National Educational Technology Standards (NETS) for Students* (ISTE, 2000) (http://cnets.iste.org/students/s_stands.html), most students indicated a low level of familiarity with them. Research on comfort in use of current technology is now underway as a first step in looking at how we can better prepare our students to transform their classroom instruction through the use of technology.

Our experience with graduate students and in-service teachers who participate in staff development workshops is that they are typically venturesome in regard to technology. It seems that if they do not know how to use an application, they ask. For a graduate class taught by the mathematics educator during a recent summer session, three of the students, all new to PowerPoint, requested a lab session in the use of this application. They were mentored in finalizing their class presentation by a sixth grader.

Ongoing Challenges

Two elements of our lives stand out as major challenges to increasing the rate at which we are able to apply technology in the improvement of teaching and learning: (a) finding the time necessary to take full advantage of the opportunities before us, and (b) working with brains that came of age with typewriters and ditto machines rather than PowerPoint and PhotoShop. We struggle to meet our own and our students' needs, constrained by the seemingly immutable and unforgiving clock. And our brains often seem not to cooperate. Although we have occasional glimpses of the transforming power of technology, we find that we must repeatedly orient–and reorient–our thinking to focus on the potential of technology in helping us accomplish our goals in teacher education. Yet we find this stage in our careers to be truly exciting, one in which continuing to negotiate the steep learning curve offers the promise of enabling us to become more effective teachers and learners through the integration of technology.

REFERENCES

Farmer, D. W. (1993). Designing a reward system to promote the career development of senior faculty. *New Directions for Teaching and Learning, 55*, 43-53.

Faseyitan, S. O., & Hirschbuhl, J. (1992). Computers in university instruction: What are the significant variables that influence adoption? *Interactive Learning International, 8*(3), 185-194.

International Society for Technology in Education (ISTE). (2000). *National educational technology standards (NETS) for students.* Retrieved November 29, 2003, from http://cnets.iste.org/students/s_stands.html

Posen, D. B. (n.d.). *Work-life balance: Setting boundaries and limits.* Retrieved November 29, 2003, from http://www.davidposen.com/pages/balance/balance2.html

Yerkes, R. M., & Dodson, J. D. (1908). The relation of strength of stimulus to rapidity of habit-formation. *Journal of Comparative Neurology and Psychology, 18*, 459-482.

APPENDIX 1

Assignment 1
Integrated Lesson (Supported by Technology)

Guidelines for the assignment:

- Plan and teach a lesson that integrates mathematics and science.
- Use technology in any way(s) that will enhance meaningful student learning.

If possible, plan a lesson that is a part of an overall project already underway in your classroom (a unit on weather, for instance).
If feasible, guide your students in preparing a technology-based presentation of their assignment.
Follow the model for lesson planning that you have been taught in class.
Reflect on your lesson according to the reflection model you have learned in class.

Note. This assignment is necessarily open so that you will be able to fit it to the curriculum and circumstances in the classroom to which you are assigned.

APPENDIX 2

Assignment 2
Use of Technology Analysis Paper

Part 1:
Select or pose a worthwhile mathematical task that is *enhanced* through the use of technology. What is your rationale for classifying the task as worthwhile? How does technology enhance the appropriateness of this task?
Select or pose a worthwhile mathematical task for which the use of technology would be *neutral*. What is your rationale for classifying the task as worthwhile? Why is technology neutral for this task?
Select or pose a worthwhile mathematical task for which the use of technology would be *inappropriate*. What is your rationale for classifying the task as worthwhile? Why is technology inappropriate for this task?
Part 2:
Summarize the criteria by which you will make decisions regarding the use of technology in your mathematics classroom.
Submit a *written report* of your analysis.

Note. This assignment was developed by Stephanie Z. Smith and Eula Ewing Monroe, mathematics educators at Brigham Young University, Provo, UT.

Roger Olsen

Electronic Portfolios in Evolution

SUMMARY. A summary of the experiences of students in one cohort at Brigham Young University is presented. The trials and errors along the journey in creating electronic portfolios are discussed. The development of electronic portfolios was an evolutionary process. Because it is an evolutionary process, adjustments will continually be made to improve the learning and growth that can take place when students create electronic portfolios. *[Article copies available for a fee from The Haworth Document Delivery Service: 1-800-HAWORTH. E-mail address: <docdelivery@haworthpress. com> Website: <http://www.HaworthPress.com> © 2004 by The Haworth Press, Inc. All rights reserved.]*

KEYWORDS. Electronic portfolio, professional development

This paper describes a dynamic process of transformation. The story began with a single university class attempting to present limited artifacts of teaching skills electronically and is now moving to the entire school of education working together to create electronic portfolios based on INTASC and ISTE standards.

Just as a horticulturist can take a wild fruit and through cross-pollination, grafting, and selective reproduction produce a wonderfully deli-

ROGER OLSEN is Liaison, Alpine Cohorts, Department of Education, Brigham Young University, Provo, UT 84602 (E-mail: roger_olsen@byu.edu).

[Haworth co-indexing entry note]: "Electronic Portfolios in Evolution." Olsen, Roger. Co-published simultaneously in *Computers in the Schools* (The Haworth Press, Inc.) Vol. 21, No. 1/2, 2004, pp. 85-94; and: *Integrating Information Technology into the Teacher Education Curriculum: Process and Products of Change* (ed: Nancy Wentworth, Rodney Earle, and Michael L. Connell) The Haworth Press, Inc., 2004, pp. 85-94. Single or multiple copies of this article are available for a fee from The Haworth Document Delivery Service [1-800-HAWORTH, 9:00 a.m. - 5:00 p.m. (EST). E-mail address: docdelivery@haworthpress.com].

Digital Object Identifier: 10.1300/J025v21n01_07

cious and beautiful fruit, so have the electronic portfolios at Brigham Young University come from a crude beginning and matured into something quite desirable. This maturation involved cross-disciplinary conversation (sometimes adding to, sometimes taking from and refining) and help from the entire McKay School of Education.

Reflective teaching is the component in the evolution of the portfolio that is valued most. A transformation in portfolio development took place as students moved from simply gathering a collection of artifacts to compiling a reflective portfolio where careful thought emerged as students studied their teaching practices and philosophies. Significant to the evolution process were the following:

1. collaboration with other faculty members,
2. ongoing conversations with small groups of students,
3. input from public school administrators and partnership facilitators,
4. technical support from the department in both equipment and personnel,
5. help from PT3 funding for training (both local and national), and
6. desire of students to create electronic portfolios.

The icing on the cake came from PT3 grant support and the kinds of assistance: training faculty and public school people through a BYU-public school partnership, training lab assistants to help students in developing electronic portfolios, bringing in advisement specialists (such as Helen Barrett), providing support for attending national conferences (SITE), and providing ongoing technical support.

Another major factor that impacted the evolution of the electronic portfolio was bringing on-board master teachers from the public schools (Clinical Faculty Associates, or CFAs) to spend two years at the university assisting in the pre-service education program. One CFA in particular brought outstanding technical skills that have had a major impact on the electronic portfolios development. Additional support and feedback came from principals who were invited to view portfolios and provide input.

CHRONOLOGY OF THE EVOLUTION

Spring 1999

A charge came from the department chair in teacher education to make technology part of the preparation of pre-service teachers. As the cohort class was not a technology class, the first challenge was to find some class requirement that could be done better with the use of technology and not just to add another assignment to the already significant student workload.

With student input, it was determined that an electronic portfolio (rather than the traditional paper portfolio) would have more appeal to pre-service students and would demonstrate a greater degree their strengths.

Summer 1999

A member of the cohort team took a class from the Alpine School District on creating electronic portfolios. The creation of what at first seemed to be a simple product became a nightmare when an attempt was made to include sound. The rendering of the file was so slow that including sound and video in the electronic portfolio seemed nearly impossible because of memory restrictions and the available hardware.

Although the task of creating electronic portfolios was initially discouraging, a vision had been created as to the benefits of such an effort. The advantages of an electronic portfolio over the paper version as envisioned at that time were: to create a portfolio that would be of interest to employers; to show the students' personality, teaching strategies, and classroom management style through video; and to showcase students' technology skills. The first attempt at electronic portfolios would best be described as a rocky road–a rocky road because there was no one else in the department doing electronic portfolios with whom to collaborate.

Fall 1999

The challenging process of developing electronic portfolios commenced with a beginning cohort of students in the Alpine School District. The idea of changing to electronic portfolios was first presented to students, and they were given the option of either continuing with the traditional paper portfolios or creating electronic portfolios. All 30 students chose to create electronic portfolios.

The categories for organizing the electronic portfolio were the same as those used with the paper version: educational philosophy, effective teaching, classroom management, the learner, diversity, personal and professional development, curriculum, assessment, and parents and community. The Alpine team had no clue as to the challenges they would face breaking new ground at the university in capturing and editing video, creating multimedia presentations, accessing hardware to compress video, and obtaining hardware to burn CDs.

Based on experiences in a class offered by the university, it was decided to use PowerPoint as the software for organizing and presenting portfolios. It was soon discovered that many of the students were unfamiliar with PowerPoint and none showed any skill in capturing and editing video. Since outside help to teach PowerPoint was not available, a team member took the PowerPoint manual and wrote a simplified step-by-step tutorial that could be used in creating the electronic portfolio.

Winter 2000

After the videotaping of 30 students teaching lessons in various partnership schools came the real challenge: How would students import the video into their portfolios? Not only were the students lacking the skills to perform the task, but the appropriate hardware was not available. Expertise from another faculty member was sought and the grueling work began for an Alpine team member to capture and compress all the video clips and burn them onto CDs for the students to include in their portfolios.

To try to determine if we were on the right course, we searched the Internet for examples of electronic portfolios with minimal success, leaving little for comparison. What we did learn from the first electronic portfolios turned in was that video and pictures greatly enhanced the visual appeal of the presentation of students' abilities. Both the format and content of the portfolios were in the initial stages of evolution. As the assistant dean and others in the department realized that electronic portfolios were really going to happen, assistance was offered in purchasing two additional digital video cameras and additional technical support.

Summer 2000

Through the PT3 grant summer workshops for faculty, team members obtained technology training in using PowerPoint and digital cameras, adding sound to presentations, and scanning, thus helping the Alpine team to feel more comfortable in assisting students with electronic portfolios.

Fall 2000

Electronic portfolios were started with a second cohort. As with the first cohort students were given the option of either the traditional paper portfolio or an electronic portfolio. Again every student chose to do an electronic portfolio.

Problems in creating the electronic portfolios experienced by the first cohort were still in place with the second cohort. One of the goals for this cohort was to give them more responsibility in capturing and editing the video before its compression. This was extremely difficult because of the availability of only one computer in the graduate lab to accomplish the task. Our students had to schedule around the graduate students' use of the computer, adding additional stress in developing electronic portfolios.

After learning of the difficulties we encountered in gaining assess to the needed hardware, the assistant dean arranged for the new computer lab under construction to be modified to help meet the needs of students compiling electronic portfolios. Five video editing stations were added to the original plans, complete with CD burners and supporting software and hardware.

A fellow professor and one of the technology support staff in the department worked with the Alpine team to train them in the use of iMovie and other software. They were also instrumental in seeing that lab assistants in the new lab would be trained to give support to our students.

Technology workshops continued to be offered by the department to give support. Conference attendees returned with ideas of what others were attempting to do with electronic portfolios.

A turning point came when one student in particular shared with faculty the insights he had gained of his own teaching strengths and weakness during the compilation of the portfolio. This identified another aspect of the process which needed to be strengthened: the need to attach meaningful reflections to each artifact. This necessary addition to the portfolio was reinforced by feedback from other professors and staff as they were shown the electronic portfolios. The focus up to this point had been in refining the technical aspects of portfolios, but after these conversations, changes were made to incorporate more reflection on the artifacts in the portfolios.

Winter 2001

A great boost came as scheduling was changed to allow a professor working on "teaching ethnographies" to teach the Alpine cohorts in an educational psychology course. Since his teaching ethnographies required students to create a CD with video clips of their teaching, they were learning skills and gathering artifacts that would be used in creating their electronic portfolios. Collaboration took place as instructors from the two courses worked together on providing experiences in the public schools to record and analyze teaching philosophies and practices of students.

During this semester the completion of the new computer lab provided students access to needed hardware and software for their electronic portfolios; however, problems still existed as computer lab assistants were not properly trained to help, and graduate students had filled up all the hard drives with their own projects. As difficult as it was, students were still successful in creating their electronic portfolios, and the workload for instructors was reduced. Portfolios produced during this semester were more reflective than from previous cohorts.

INTASC standards were presented to the education faculty as the standards the state would be using for new teacher licensure. They were then introduced to the students as a possible framework for organizing their portfolios. This was the beginning of a shift from the local expectations to teaching standards (INTASC) more widely recognized throughout the country.

Examples of electronic portfolios from the cohorts were shown to all 38 principals in the Alpine School District. The purpose was to see if principals would be interested in viewing electronic portfolios as part of the hiring process for new teachers. (Previously principals had not shown interest in seeing paper portfolios.) When given a questionnaire regarding interest in viewing electronic portfolios as part of the hiring process, all principals said they would like to view the electronic portfolios when interviewing.

Two members of the Alpine team attended the SITE conference in Orlando along with other department faculty. At that conference, another milestone in the evolutionary process occurred. Helen Barrett opened their vision to the deeper, more encompassing purposes of electronic portfolios. To this point, portfolios produced by cohorts were collections of artifacts with some reflections added. It was evident that previous efforts at producing portfolios had focused on creating presentation portfolios for prospective employers. Working portfolios, with the tremendous opportunities they afford students to evaluate their practices and philosophies, had not been given adequate emphasis. It was determined while at the SITE conference to invite Helen Barrett to do a workshop at Brigham Young University for the faculty in the McKay School of Education.

The leadership in the McKay School of Education had by this time committed effort and resources to make it possible for education majors to do electronic portfolios. Because of this commitment, the Alpine team presented samples of electronic portfolios to faculty and other leaders responsible for the cohort program. This group seemed impressed with the electronic portfolios; however, most felt they were not ready to attempt electronic portfolios because of inadequacy with technical skills. To address concerns and assist in the creation of electronic portfolios a task force was formed. This task force began a dialogue with those who teach the technology courses and other faculty to build a support system for students to create portfolios electronically.

Summer 2001

Helen Barrett worked with the faculty for three days, giving instruction in the purpose of portfolios and how they can be enhanced electronically. Her instruction would prove to be a milestone in refining and emphasizing the purpose of the working portfolio.

Fall 2001

The purpose of the portfolio had now evolved (as desired by the Alpine team) to be built upon the INTASC standards with ideas from Helen Barrett added to what had already been done. As the fall cohort had already spent a semester working on their portfolios, they were not required to change the structure of what they had started, but invited to make the change if desired. Fifteen of the 23 students expressed the desire to change to the INTASC standards and incorporate some of Helen Barrett's ideas. A high point of the semester was the students' enthusiasm as they caught a vision of what the portfolio could do for them to show evidence that they were meeting standards.

Students who desired were invited to meet with the instructors beyond class time to collaborate on developing electronic portfolios. Students were anxious to meet to share ideas, ask questions, and get feedback. It was difficult to describe the energy and enthusiasm of the group as they realized ownership of their portfolios. Much of the energy seemed to come as students realized that their ideas were valued as much as those of the instructors. They moved from merely collecting artifacts to gathering evidence of their teaching skills.

Some BYU faculty and teams from the partnership districts traveled together to the Classroom Connect conference in Las Vegas for the purpose of building cohesion in the technology skills taught at the university and those needed by classroom teachers. Many benefits came from the conference, but one in particular was the district support for electronic portfolios. As the majority of the new teachers in the Alpine School District come from BYU, the district teams were excited to learn of the skills that the graduates would bring to the district. They expressed their support in continuing electronic portfolios with those new teachers for the purpose of collecting evidence to meet licensure requirements during their first two years of teaching.

Administrators from the Alpine District met with students and viewed their electronic portfolios. Involving the administrators had a twofold purpose. The main objective was to provide feedback to the students from a public school perspective. Another objective was to evaluate the portfolios in general to see if they actually showed (from an administrator's perspective) evidence of INTASC standards being met.

Winter 2002-03

Partnership facilitators from the Alpine School District became more heavily involved in evaluating the electronic portfolios against INTASC standards. Each semester the portfolios generally became more reflective and better at showing growth in the teaching abilities of cohort students.

An action research project evolved from the question of "How well do the electronic portfolios show evidence of pre-service teachers meeting INTASC standards?" A CFA from the Alpine School District gathered the data. This required creating a rubric so that all who evaluated the portfolios (both BYU faculty and public school people) would evaluate from the same perspective.

In order to make the evaluations more reliable (even with a rubric) all those who would evaluate the portfolios were brought together and trained in use of the rubric. Students showed evidence of meeting the INTASC standards through a collection of:

- Artifacts: lesson plans, management plans, evidence of learning plans, video clips of teaching, reflections on readings and assignments, and teaching episodes.
- Reproductions: copies of works produced by their students, videos of student productions and projects, and audios of student progress.
- Attestations: letters of recommendations, observation by peers and supervisors, certificates of completion of workshops.

Figures 1 and 2 are samples showing the degree to which evaluators saw the INTASC standards being met from the students' collection of artifacts, reproductions, and attestations.

FIGURE 1. Evidence of cohort's meeting INTASC standard 5 (management) during their Elementary Education 302 experience.

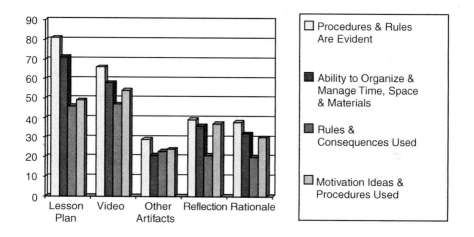

FIGURE 2. Evidence of cohort's meeting INTASC standards 1 and 7 (content pedagogy and planning) during their Elementary Education 302 experience.

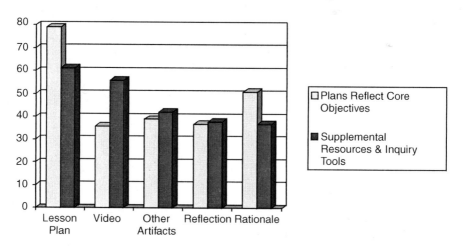

The Evolution Continues

We continue to refine both the design and the implementation of electronic portfolios. Our experiences during the past few years, despite the challenges both technically and conceptually, have strengthened our resolve and our attestation that electronic portfolios provide our pre-service students with effective means to document, chart, and analyze their professional growth and development. We have learned much. We have much more to learn. We continue our quest with the same enthusiasm exhibited by the horticulturist using cross-pollination, grafting, and selective reproduction to produce a wonderfully delicious and beautiful fruit. We see that our students are refining the electronic portfolios at Brigham Young University, though crude initially, into something quite desirable.

Carol Lee Hawkins
Sharon Black

Developing Electronic Portfolios Across the State of Utah: Breaks, Breakdowns and Breakthroughs

SUMMARY. When Brigham Young University received a PT3 grant three years ago, the university, the Utah State Office of Education, and individual school districts throughout the state were just beginning to explore possible benefits and implementation strategies for electronic portfolios. With a few fortunate "breaks"–financial, administrative, and technological–all of these groups began to think about electronic portfolios more seriously. Although there were some breakdowns and near breakdowns, caused by initial isolation of efforts and suspicion among participants, these groups learned to trust and collaborate, resulting in breakthroughs, as models, expert guidance, and implementation opportunities were offered and progress was achieved. At present, statewide collaborative efforts are enabling BYU, the State Office of Education, and districts and teacher preparation institutions to pass "breaks" for-

CAROL LEE HAWKINS is Special Assistant to the Dean, David O. McKay School of Education, Brigham Young University, Provo, UT 84602 (E-mail: carol_lee_hawkins@ byu.edu).
SHARON BLACK is Associate Professor, Department of Teacher Education, Brigham Young University, Provo, UT 84602 (E-mail: Sharon_black@byu.edu).

[Haworth co-indexing entry note]: "Developing Electronic Portfolios Across the State of Utah: Breaks, Breakdowns and Breakthroughs." Hawkins, Carol Lee, and Sharon Black. Co-published simultaneously in *Computers in the Schools* (The Haworth Press, Inc.) Vol. 21, No. 1/2, 2004, pp. 95-113; and: *Integrating Information Technology into the Teacher Education Curriculum: Process and Products of Change* (ed: Nancy Wentworth, Rodney Earle, and Michael L. Connell) The Haworth Press, Inc., 2004, pp. 95-113. Single or multiple copies of this article are available for a fee from The Haworth Document Delivery Service [1-800-HAWORTH, 9:00 a.m. - 5:00 p.m. (EST). E-mail address: docdelivery@haworthpress.com].

Digital Object Identifier: 10.1300/J025v21n01_08

ward to pre-service and in-service teachers, including an instruction/support sequence, a layered model that includes both working and presentation portfolios, and free lifetime server space provided by the Utah Education Network. In this article the authors share the journey and map the current point of arrival. *[Article copies available for a fee from The Haworth Document Delivery Service: 1-800-HAWORTH. E-mail address: <docdelivery@haworthpress.com> Website: <http://www.HaworthPress.com> © 2004 by The Haworth Press, Inc. All rights reserved.]*

KEYWORDS. Electronic portfolio, working portfolio, statewide collaboration

In our enthusiasm for a PT3 grant to infuse technology into pre-service teacher preparation and in-service teacher support, we made an optimistic promise: "One thousand graduating Brigham Young University education students per year will produce an electronic portfolio documenting their understanding of designing and implementing technology-rich curriculum." This seemed unbelievable to many, since as of June 2000, when we received the PT3 grant, the McKay School of Education had produced only 28 electronic portfolios. As a member of the oldest, continually functioning, university-public school partnership in the nation, Brigham Young University had qualified and experienced strong relationships with talented and highly trained technology specialists in five school districts, and positive ties with an enthusiastic and capable staff at the Utah State Office of Education. Surely producing portfolios was a natural step for this group. But was it? And was a goal of 3,000 portfolios in three years even a possibility?

"Yes" and "no" answers to these questions have been bandied around quite a bit during the three years of BYU's PT3 undertaking. Ideally, we would have made a clear and reasonable plan and moved inexorably toward success. Realistically, we've had several fortunate breaks, a number of discouraging breakdowns, and some exciting breakthroughs. These have culminated in our being able to offer a number of helpful and empowering "breaks" for pre-service students and entry-years practitioners in assembling electronic portfolios with the potential to add immeasurably to their professional development and documentation. This chapter will share our process.

BREAKS

We began the portfolio aspect of our PT3 involvement with a number of "breaks" in our favor. In addition to the expanded funding contributed by the grant, we had a state office that was in the process of creating a program to enhance the experience of novice teachers, a state educational network that had connected every classroom in Utah to the Internet, and a university School of Education that was altering its assessment measures to correspond with national changes as reflected in the NCATE requirements. Separately, perhaps these factors would have resulted in minor, short-term changes that would have affected individual groups and institutions at best. Together, these fortuitous breaks were to have far-reaching consequences for all of us.

Break 1: Early Years Enhancement (EYE)

At the time BYU was developing PT3 plans to enhance its preparation of teachers, the Utah State Office of Education was developing plans to enhance its support of entry-level teachers. Regularly scheduled mentoring and administrator evaluations were to be required, along with necessary preparation for the Praxis II examination as the new teachers approached their third year and would require Level II licensure. Portfolios were under consideration as a further requirement, but practical considerations were not being quickly resolved. Electronic portfolios had been suggested, but had not received the widespread support they would need. The State Office was looking for solutions.

Break 2: Utah Educational Network (UEN)

While BYU, as the state's largest teacher-preparation institution, was searching for ways to infuse technology into the teacher preparation curriculum, and the State Office was contemplating use of technology in supporting teachers, the Utah Education Network (UEN) was busy preparing curriculum technology resources for teachers to use. UEN has described itself as the "one-stop URL for Utah educators" (Richard Gaisford, *training workshop*, October 2000). By providing hardware, instruction, and Web space over the past decade, UEN had succeeded in building a virtual community for all Utah educators by bringing the Internet to every classroom and teacher in the state. UEN was encouraging teachers statewide to expand their curriculum and teaching techniques via the Internet, to enhance their technology skills, and to create, store, and share their multimedia presentations. This group had both the knowledge and the resources to integrate technological developments statewide.

Break 3: BYU and NCATE

At this time BYU's School of Education was looking at significant changes in assessment as well as classroom technology. Attention nationwide was shifting toward competency-based assessment, and standards newly adopted by NCATE were requiring work in that direction. Administrators and assessment specialists were searching for ways to provide evidence of their students' learning and development. This group needed the precision and systemization that technology could provide, along with the perspective and statewide connections held by the other groups.

These diverse groups shared a goal: better preparation and support of teachers, with current emphasis on technology. With their overlapping interests and needs–along with varied personnel and resources, knowledge and skills–both breakdowns and breakthroughs would inevitably occur.

BREAKDOWNS AND NEAR BREAKDOWNS

Although the State of Utah had within its varied organizations the knowledge, resources, personnel, connections, skills, and, above all, the recognition of needs that could make those 3,000 portfolios reality, in August 2000 too many things were breaking down and incomplete. The goal of implementing widespread electronic portfolios seemed impossible.

Isolation

Despite the common overreaching goal to prepare and support teachers, each organization, group, or entity had its own goals and its own agenda. The EYE project was focusing on the requirements for Level II licensure of its teachers. UEN was focusing on connecting, collecting, and disseminating–on getting technological resources to those teachers. BYU was focusing on giving its pre-service teachers a course in using basic technology, trying to convince faculty to infuse and model technology, and searching for ways to demonstrate that both were being accomplished. Words like *electronic portfolio* were tossed into the mix from time to time, but these groups did not have a common vision of what electronic portfolios were or how they could be developed.

Suspicions and Fears

Experiences of institutions that have implemented electronic portfolios have shown consistently that support and participation by the faculty is key to development and implementation (Gathercoal, Love, Bryde, & McKean, 2002; Rainy River, 2002; Winsor, 1998). Groups within the BYU faculty were becoming enthusiastic about technology integration and were beginning to use the "P word" more confidently–particularly in content areas such as art, social studies, and language arts. Groups of administrative and peripheral personnel, such as computer lab and grant administrators, were meeting and providing input as well. Dr. Rodney Earle, Associate Chair of the Department of Teacher Education, agreed to work with a select group of faculty to explore the development of a department program portfolio, and his group was looking into different possibilities.

But the greater part of the BYU School of Education faculty were suspicious regarding the amount of time and effort that would be required to infuse technology into their carefully honed courses and teaching styles. Students were hearing inconsistent comments and seeing a variety of faculty behavior regarding technology generally and electronic portfolios specifically. Like the faculty, students guarded their time and uncertain expertise defensively. A catalyst was needed to get the groups and the individuals aligned and functioning purposefully.

BREAKTHROUGHS

As the PT3 grant was a financial catalyst for the development of technology integration and eventually electronic portfolios, BYU's first involvement with PT3 gatherings was a conceptual catalyst for these operations. On June 25, 2000, Carol Lee Hawkins, a grant administrator from BYU, and Steve Soulier, a professor of instructional science from Utah State University–a fellow grant recipient, attended the annual PT3 general meeting in Atlanta as representatives of their institutions. At this series of meetings, Hawkins and Soulier developed a panoramic vision of how electronic portfolios might be developed and implemented and what they might eventually contribute to education and educators in the State of Utah.

This first breakthrough was followed by others, many at unexpected times and from varied participants. From as far away as Alaska and as close to home as BYU-public school liaisons, people brought a wide range of skills, experiences, talents, and connections to the portfolio experience.

From the East Coast: Examples of Successful Initiatives

As Hawkins and Soulier sat in the Atlanta meetings, they became more and more excited over what other institutions were doing with their PT3 grants. Their enthusiasm peaked as the Virginia consortium explained how they had developed a dynamic statewide operation, with regular monthly meetings and cross-institutional collaboration. Realizing that Utah had the technology facilities, the personnel, and the formal collaborative structures to do something comparable, they decided to meet periodically through the tenure of the grant to share research and discuss portfolio development.

The next step where Ms. Hawkins was concerned was to do research. After intensive online reading and correspondence, she visited five universities in North Carolina that were showing impressive results with their programs. All five were preparing pre-service teachers for a statewide licensing requirement that they successfully demonstrate their competency in basic and advanced technology skills, documenting their accomplishments with an electronic portfolio. She observed what resources these universities had, how they used their resources, and how they involved their faculties. Returning to BYU, she reported that BYU had technology facilities that were superior to those of any of the universities she had visited. What these universities had that BYU lacked were committed faculty and strong, active central university support and training. With ample support and instruction available to them, faculty at the universities in North Carolina were using technology in their own courses, including technology skills in the assignments they gave their students, and creating opportunities for students to demonstrate their skills. These components did not seem to Ms. Hawkins to be beyond what BYU administrators and faculty should be able to do.

From Alaska: Dr. Helen Barrett

With some background on successful electronic portfolio programs, BYU personnel turned to one of the most successful producers of electronic portfolio content and instruction: Dr. Helen Barrett of the University of Alaska. Conversations began at a Society for Information Technology and Teacher Education (SITE) conference in March 2001, and Dr. Barrett was persuaded to conduct workshops for a mixed group consisting of administrators and professors from three Utah universities; public school district teachers, administrators, and technology specialists; and state office personnel. After two days of workshops in June of 2001, including several sessions consisting of collaborative small-group interaction, Helen Barrett and the State of Utah were synergistically bonded. Dr. Barrett declared, "I will stick with Utah if you want me!" She designated the small-group collaborative workshop model as her "BYU Model."

When Helen Barrett returned to Utah a year later, a group gathered to work with her at Utah State University, consisting of representatives from five universities and the Utah Education Network (UEN) in addition to the Utah State Office of Education and school district representatives. Dr. Barrett has remained a close friend and advisor to the groups of Utah educators throughout the portfolio development process. Her coaching and influence have taught us much about what portfolios should look and sound like, and her feedback and encouragement have been instrumental in moving us forward as we have designed the portfolio program that we are initiating today.

From Nebo School District: Nancy Evenson and the Nebo Cohort

Faculty from all departments in the School of Education attended Helen Barrett's workshop. Many who had been timid, hesitant, or suspicious about electronic portfolios became interested, if not enthusiastic, in learning what could be accomplished and how doable this seemed to be. But someone had to lead out–to actually introduce electronic portfolios to the pre-service teachers and persuade them to participate.

Nancy Evenson, district liaison for the Nebo School District in the BYU Partnership, was given copies of some of Helen Barrett's materials. On vacation, Nancy Evenson became so enthusiastic that, while her family relaxed on the beach, she read about reflection and portfolios. By the end of her vacation she was converted, and by the time school started up again in the fall she had agreed to introduce electronic portfolios to the cohort of pre-service students she was supervising as they prepared for their first in-school practicum experience.

Ms. Evenson laid down some groundwork for her students' participation: (a) to prepare an electronic portfolio in place of the paper portfolio she usually required was to be strictly voluntary, (b) students who elected to do the electronic version would receive ample instruction and technical support, (c) electronic portfolios should not increase the workload of her students, (d) time spent dealing with electronic portfolios should not compromise the curriculum of her course, and, perhaps of greatest importance, (e) the Nebo School District administration must support and sustain the portfolio initiative. The electronic portfolio group and the district agreed.

During the first semester that electronic portfolios were offered as an option in Nancy Evenson's course, seven students volunteered. Student tutors at the School of Education's Teaching and Learning Support Center (computer lab) assisted in producing templates and tutorials to help them, and supplied one-on-one guidance as the students worked through production processes. With input from Evenson, several teaching assistants, and Nebo School District administrators, Carol Lee Hawkins developed a basic working portfolio format, which included an Excel spreadsheet for organization and access, based on the INTASC standards with hypertext links to artifacts and reflective statements. The experiment was underway. The students required less instruction than had been anticipated.

As the seven student volunteers completed their electronic portfolios, they couldn't help noticing that their roommates and friends who were doing the traditional paper portfolios were spending much more time and money. Some of the students noted that with the time they saved they were able to put more effort into revising and reflecting on their work. All agreed that they preferred the electronic portfolio.

One of the portfolio volunteers affirmed:

> This was a positive experience, even though I was nervous and unsure of myself technologically at first.

Another praised efficiency of the system:

> What I really, really like about it is that it's just so organized. . . . I can click on my hyperlink that I created and it just brings it up.

Another of the students showed insight into the long-range value of what she was doing:

> I think it also shows just that you collect a lot of things . . . that you want to look at your things, you want to reflect on them. I think

that's a really important thing for teaching: You need to reflect on your things. And having them as artifacts, you'll reflect on them.

At the end of the school year, Ms. Evenson and others who supervised and worked with practicum students in the Nebo School District agreed that from that point on electronic portfolios would be required.

From Around the State of Utah:
More Institutions, Administrative Groups, and Individuals

The Utah State Office of Education continued to work on the program of Early Years Enhancement (EYE) for its beginning teachers. After participating in the workshops with Helen Barrett, State Office participants found their understanding of portfolios was developing beyond the stage of concept, as they were understanding ways that portfolios could be used to strengthen teaching and learning. As the leader of the EYE project, Dr. Stanfield, wrote:

> A whole new world of technical support for teachers was opened. The enthusiasm of the presentation and the interest among the individuals attending was contagious, giving rise to a spontaneous interchange of ideas. The three Utah institutions working with PT3 grants . . . established a committee of interested partners including Utah Education Network, districts, and Utah State Office of Education personnel to study the possibility of using portfolios as an enhancement to assess new teachers' skills. (Personal Communication, 2003)

In March 2002 a Utah Higher Education Portfolio Working Group was established, chaired by Carol Lee Hawkins with additional leadership from Kathleen Webb of the State Office and Dr. Richard Cline from the Utah Education Network. The archive spreadsheet was adopted, and the tutorials developed for the Nebo District were extended and refined.

As the electronic portfolio initiative gained momentum statewide, Ms. Webb shared the model extensively and obtained funding for a pilot test involving groups throughout Utah. Dr. Cline worked with UEN and obtained their commitment to provide 100 MG of no-cost storage space for every pre-service teacher in the state. In addition, UEN agreed to extend this archival service to all teachers in Utah and sustain it so that pre-service teachers can create a portfolio during their university years, continue to own and build it as they enter district employment, and strengthen and revise it as they move from district to district throughout their careers.

In January 2003, Utah's new Level II Licensure requirements became law. Included among them was the specification that all candidates must develop portfolios and participate in a mentoring program. Faculty and staff from 41 districts and 7 universities attended training conducted by state and university personnel to prepare them to instruct and scaffold pre-service and in-service teachers in preparing electronic portfolios. Instruction on the portfolios, along with an accompanying mentoring program, emphasized the INTASC standards, on which the portfolios were to be based. Processes of reflection were introduced as well.

Teacher preparation programs are supporting the electronic portfolio effort. Five colleges and universities throughout the state have adopted the portfolio model, including the spreadsheet that was originally drawn up for the BYU/Nebo School District cohort. At BYU, 400 students in the required technology course are currently participating in the statewide pilot of the program, developing an Excel-based working portfolio as part of their course assignments. In addition, some sections of an English course taken by BYU elementary and early childhood education majors are experimenting with specific instruction and assignments in reflective writing, compiling a number of the course assignments into a "reflective portfolio" on which the students receive fairly extensive coaching and feedback. With this guidance and instruction, along with the server space donated by UEN, pre-service teachers are getting a good start on meeting the portfolio requirement.

Through conferences, presentations, workshops, and other meetings on institutional, local, and state levels, a variety of ideas, methodologies, and strategies are being shared. As Dr. Stanfield, the Coordinator of Educational Licensing for the state, has written, "Members of PT3 grants . . . school districts, and the State Office of Education have all collaborated to actualize the use of electronic portfolios. The project has evolved from total ignorance to full implementation by professional educators in Utah" (Personal Communication, 2003). Participants in the educational enterprise throughout the State of Utah were by this time united in supporting pre-service and in-service teachers in developing electronic portfolios.

BREAKS PASSED FORWARD

Fortunate breaks have been maximized, breakdowns have been patched (and sometimes deconstructed and re-patched), and breakthroughs have emerged. As a result, we are able to pass new fortunate breaks on to pre-service and early-years teachers both at BYU and throughout the State of Utah.

A New Perspective

In the past, most pre-service (and many in-service) teachers have considered a "portfolio" to be a scrapbook-like collection of their flashiest, most colorful work, pasted onto acid-free paper, embellished with stickers and other illustrations, and submitted in a loose-leaf binder to a professor for a grade at the end of a course. Another year, another course, another collection. When words like *electronic* and *professional* are attached, students may find the designations unsettling. Does this mean clip art instead of stickers and a zip disk instead of a binder? If they are going to produce a professional electronic portfolio for Level II licensure, these college students and first-year teachers need a new way to conceptualize what their portfolio should be like, what it should accomplish, and when and how they should go about doing it.

Part of this reconceptualization can be beneficially structured around the definition of *portfolio* provided by Campbell, Cignetti, Melenyzer, Nettles, and Wyman (2001): "A portfolio is an organized, goal-driven documentation of your professional growth and achieved competence in the complex act called teaching" (p. 3).

Growth in professional knowledge and competence does not occur overnight—it occurs over time. A student enters a pre-service teaching preparation program with certain strengths and potentials, which are refined and developed during the subsequent two or three years of training. To document this growth—particularly in an organized and goal-driven manner—the student must provide evidence of advancing levels of competency. The portfolio does not merely skim off the senior student's most recent production. Thus artifacts must be selected and preserved from the beginning of the program, and a student must be aware from the beginning of the competencies in which the growth will be assessed. The program that we use at Brigham Young University and throughout Utah views the portfolio as a representation that develops and improves over a teacher's entire professional life. We attempt to guide our prospective and practicing teachers as they learn to conceptualize portfolios according to this potential. But we also provide broad opportunity for individual application and expression. To orient and guide those who are preparing portfolios, we have worked out a flexible system, including a model which is easy to apply for both technology and content, along with provisions for continuity and continuation.

A Model with Support

Acknowledging the need for structure and professionalism, program designers chose to have the portfolios built around the INTASC standards, with which district and State standards had already been aligned. At BYU, students who have been accepted to the teacher preparation program attend an initial orientation session in which they are introduced both to an overview of electronic portfolios and to the content and application of the INTASC standards. In many of their teacher preparation courses, instruction is focused on relevant INTASC standards; and assignments, when possible, are structured to provide some potential artifacts to go into portfolios. Creation of individual portfolio artifacts is based on experiences of individual purpose and expression; students are provided the INTASC standards to formulate bases for these artifacts, and they receive process and/or product feedback when appropriate.

We developed the electronic storage system to be initiated as an introductory Excel assignment in the Teaching with Technology course and to be sustained and expanded throughout the program. Thus faculty whose courses do not focus on technology can be secure that their course content will not be compromised by the necessity of teaching technological processes and issues relating to the electronic portfolio.

If the portfolio is to be an individual's creative work, representing his or her professional development and progress, it must be owned by the individual who creates it, not by an institution or a district. Thus the portfolio has to stored so that only the teacher has complete access. But in formulating the program we also wanted to create opportunities for teachers to share materials, work collaboratively, and obtain feedback from peers, mentors, and supervisors. And, in addition, we felt the need for a public arena to share and publish materials for general audiences. Purchase of an Apple Universal Locker System by UEN provided the differential access necessary for these varied opportunities, also the possibility of easily accessing the portfolio over the Internet from any location at no cost to the teachers.

In addition to the flexibility necessary to provide for differences among individual teachers, we recognized the importance of providing flexibility for the teachers themselves among portfolio uses and purposes that they will experience over their careers.

A Layered Portfolio System

A portfolio that is ideal for exiting a pre-service program may well be inadequate for a later professional advancement. Thus we decided on a flexible system whereby the teacher would collect a variety of work in an *archive*; reflect on selected pieces, according to INTASC standards, and place them in a *working portfolio*; and when an occasion should necessitate a portfolio for a specific purpose and audience, be capable of quickly and easily compiling a *presentation portfolio* (see Figure 1).

Working portfolio. Pre-service teachers at BYU register at UEN and set up a storage and access system for a *working portfolio* as they take a beginning educational technology course during the first year of their professional sequence. This working portfolio will be a place to store a varied collection of artifacts from which students may draw when they are assigned by professors, mentors, administrators, or prospective employers to prepare a specialized performance portfolio for a specific time and purpose. Campbell, Cignetti, Melenyzer, Nettles, and Wyman (2001) refer to the working portfolio as the "unabridged version" of a person's work (p. 3). Kimball (2003) explains its use:

> A working portfolio isn't usually subjected to direct assessment: it contains more material than the author would want to show anyone, and the material isn't necessarily revised for people to see. However, a working portfolio is carefully organized and maintained so when the time comes to create a more formal portfolio, the material will be ready at hand. (p. 8)

FIGURE 1. The layered portfolio model designed for the BYU program.

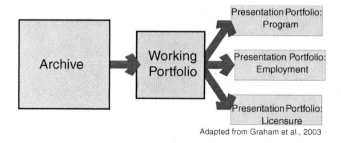

Adapted from Graham et al., 2003

Students are taught how to create a spreadsheet that organizes their work according to the INTASC standards that it represents. Since one piece of work may include several standards, the sample spreadsheet, which is offered but not required as a template, is set up with INTASC standards on the horizontal axis, with additional relevant sets of standards that correspond with them indicated as well (see Figure 2).

The artifacts that students wish to place in the portfolio are listed vertically, and links are created on the spreadsheet for all standards with which the piece of work may be considered.

Thus if a student wishes to include a thematic unit plan that illustrates her ability to consider student development, provide for the learning

FIGURE 2. Sample spreadsheet given to students as a model for organizing the working portfolio.

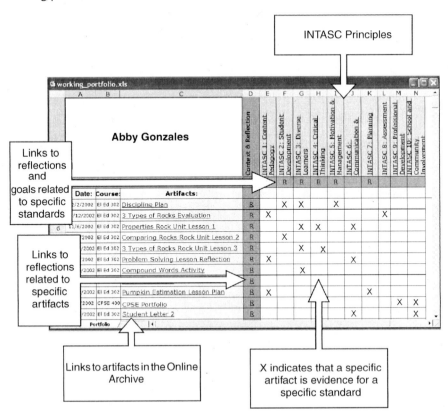

styles of diverse learners, and use a variety of instructional methods, while promoting strong motivation and at the same time providing effective presentation of important content, links provided opposite that unit plan might be placed at five points if the student wishes the work to represent all five of those INTASC categories. Because the free storage space provided by UEN can be accessed at any time and placed throughout the teacher's eventual career and can be revised or removed at any time, students are encouraged to keep a wide range of products, including some that show weaknesses for the sake of comparing and showing progress.

Students are given the option to use the template illustrated in Figure 2 or to set up their own comparable archive for keeping their work organized and accessible. The introductory technology course instructor presents the process during class; then students go to the Teaching and Learning Support Center where they prepare their portfolio, with tutorials to remind them of the process and lab assistants to help them.

Presentation portfolios. Throughout BYU's teacher preparation program, various instructors require their students to submit *course portfolios*. At specific pivotal points in the program, Department of Teacher Education administrators request *program portfolios*, demonstrating particular competencies that should be demonstrable at those times. As they participate in practicum experiences in the schools, some will submit *mentoring portfolios* on which those who are assigned to mentor and assess them will be able to base discussion. As they exit the program, *an exit portfolio* reflecting their entire program will be required. And, of course, some post-graduation interviews and mentoring and all Level II licensure will require still different portfolios. These are just the predictable *presentation portfolios* that teachers emerging from BYU's program will need to prepare. Numerous other uses and applications will probably follow many of them throughout their teaching careers. If the materials in the working portfolio are created, reflected upon, revised, and stored carefully, items specified for and appropriate to presentation portfolios can be easily selected, extracted, and organized for each occasion, purpose, and audience.

LESSONS FROM OUR BREAKS AND BREAKDOWNS

In the process of breaking in our electronic portfolio program, we have learned some lessons and gained some insights that will impact future development and administration of our program. We have found we need to focus on administration, faculty, and students in order to make our program beneficial. This summary of our lessons will be organized according to these groups.

Administration

In developing administrative policies and practices concerning electronic portfolios, we have found it especially important to ensure that producing the portfolios is an integral aspect of our teacher preparation program. In our initial experience in the Nebo School District, we began the portfolio application early in the program, as pre-service teachers were preparing for their initial fieldwork. We have found through the Nebo experience that the portfolio can be effectively used as formative assessment, and that it can be a valuable tool for mentoring of both pre-service and first-year teachers. So successful was the combination of portfolio and mentoring, that Nebo District was able to obtain a $360,000 grant to set up a mentoring program based on electronic portfolios. This program is now in operation, with positive results.

In making the portfolios integral to the program, we have found it valuable for the students to receive instruction, modeling, and support in setting up their working portfolios during the course in educational technology that is required near the beginning of their program. We have found that when constructing the spreadsheet and organizing portfolio materials is an assignment for the course, students do it in a timely and efficient manner. It is also easier to provide the technical support when students are coming to lab at specified times of the semester for the particular tutorials and help from laboratory assistants. Communication between the lab director and the professor for the course has been positive and productive. The carefully trained staff at the lab understands the program requirements and the goals and specifications of the faculty, as well as the technological aspects of the selected electronic portfolio system.

Faculty

Gathercoal, Love, Bryde and McKean (2002) reported on their experience with electronic portfolios:

> Our experiences indicate that a critical success factor for electronic portfolio implementation is a culture where faculty understand their central role in the portfolio process as resource providers, mentors, conveyors of standards, and definers of qual-

ity. The major obstacle to successful implementation of Web-based electronic portfolios is not student readiness, it is full faculty participation. We have met the enemy . . . and the enemy is us. (p. 30)

Our experience has been similar. Some university faculty have been enthusiastic about the development of electronic portfolios, and their students have been successful. But the program overall has moved slowly when faculty have been hesitant–suspicious that their curriculum, their preferred teaching style, and/or their students' time for class study will be compromised by the time required for ongoing portfolio development. BYU's climate for participation is a major focus of our work at this time. Presently we are finding more enthusiasm among the Utah State Office of Education, Utah Education Network, and school district personnel than we have had among the university faculty. We are slowly improving our own climate; it seems to be getting more positive as the program becomes more tightly organized and the students are receiving more consistent instruction. As portfolios become more and more integral to the program, we are seeing faculty becoming more involved and taking more responsibility.

Students

The more important participants and beneficiaries of the electronic portfolio program must be the students. To have the function we desire of them, electronic portfolios must be student-centered, student-owned, and student-friendly. For the portfolio to be student-centered, the student must be the designer, the artist, and the technician. Although faculty, administrators, and lab assistants can and should model and instruct in the process and should demonstrate options for content, the final decisions as to portfolio design, artifact selection, and the reflection process must be made by the students themselves, representing the individual student's strengths, values, talents, goals, and skills. Although they receive instruction on the INTASC standards within the context of their pre-service courses, the way students interpret and apply these standards and represent them in artifacts and reflections must be their own.

For the portfolios to be student-owned, the student must be able to control access–sharing what is desired when it is desired and with whom. There must be some places in the portfolio that are private, reserved for projects in development or experimentation, for products that may be flawed but the source of learning and revision. There must be places available only to trusted mentors or close friends; other places where evaluators, assessors, or prospective employers may visit. The Universal Locker furnished by UEN is proving ideal for this sort of ownership.

The portfolio must also be student-friendly. We've found that low-end, inexpensive technology works bests for large groups of pre-service teachers. Pre-service teachers must have confidence that the computer will not corrupt their portfolio, lose important work, or present barriers to quick and easy storage of materials or to later free access to them.

CONCLUSION

Kilbane and Milman (2003) note that both the National Board for Professional Teaching Standards (NBPTS) and Interstate New Teachers Assessment and Support Consortium (INTASC) support teaching portfolios as "an authentic means for demonstrating the many facets of a teacher's professionalism" and "the best method of illustrating an individual teacher's attainment of certain professional standards" (Kilbane & Milman, p. 7). With such endorsements by highly respected and influential teacher development groups, there has been a pervasive trend for states to implement requirements for professional portfolios–especially electronic portfolios–in programs for teacher assessment, licensure, and employment. The State of Utah has joined this movement, adopting in 2003 the requirement of a portfolio as one of the main criteria for Level II licensure. With funding and support from the BYU 2000-2003 PT3 grant, a group consisting of PT3 administrators, university faculty, school district personnel, and state education leaders had the opportunity to design, develop, and implement a statewide electronic portfolio system, which is currently being pilot tested by teachers in several districts and by faculty at six Utah colleges and universities: Brigham Young University, the University of Utah, Salt Lake Community College, Utah Valley State College, Southern Utah University, and Dixie State College. We anticipate that collaboration and frequent assessment will be key to its continuing success.

Our progress toward developing and implementing a statewide program for electronic professional portfolios has not been a smooth upward curve. We have had a lot of fortuitous breaks, a few breakdowns and near breakdowns, and some exciting breakthroughs on the university, local, and state levels. As a result, we've been able to offer some empowering breaks for Utah's future teachers. Our program is moving forward.

At the beginning of our PT3 grant, we committed optimistically to produce 3,000 portfolios in three years. Many thought that we, as faculty, staff, and students at BYU, would not be able to do this. They were both right and wrong in this prediction. They acknowledged our weaknesses, but they failed to acknowledge our allies in the public school districts, the Utah State Office of Education, the Utah Educational Network, and our sister colleges and universities. As Brigham Young University, we have not yet produced 3,000 portfolios. But as the State of Utah, we have!

REFERENCES

Campbell, D.M., Cignetti, P.B., Melenyzer, B.J., Nettles, D.H., & Wyman, R.M. (2001). *How to develop a professional portfolio: A manual for teachers* (2nd ed.). Boston: Allyn & Bacon.

Gaisford, R. (2000, October). *Training workshop.* Salt Lake City, UT: Utah State Office of Education.

Gathercoal, P., Love, D., Bryde, B., & McKean, G. (2002). On implementing Web-based electronic portfolios. *Educause Quarterly, 2,* 30. Retrieved October 7, 2003, from http://www.educause.edu/ir/library/pdf/eqm0224.pdf.

Ghaye, A., & Ghaye, K. (1998). *Teaching and learning through critical reflective practice.* London: David Fulton Publishers.

Graham, C.R., Webb, K., Hawkins, C.L., & Harlan, D. (2003). Linking mentoring and electronic teaching portfolios for Utah educators. *Journal of UASCD Theories & Practices in Supervision and Curriculum, XIV,* 59-66.

Kilbane, C.R., & Milman, N.B. (2003). *The digital teaching portfolio handbook: A how to guide for educators.* New York: Pearson Education.

Kimball, M.A. (2003). *The Web portfolio guide.* New York: Longman.

Rainy River Community College (2002). *Electronic portfolios: Documenting student academic achievement.* Final Report. Unpublished manuscript.

Winsor, P. (1998). *A guide to the development of professional portfolios in faculty education.* Retrieved October 21, 2003, from http://www.edu.uleth.ca/fe/pdf/portfolio_guide.pdf.

Wyatt, R.L. III, & Looper, S. (1999). *So you have to have a portfolio: A teacher's guide to preparation and presentation.* Thousand Oaks, CA: Corwin Press.

J. Aaron Popham
Rebecca Rocque

Faculty-as-Students: Teacher Education Faculty Meaningfully Engaged in a Pre-Service Technology Course

SUMMARY. This study looked at a different approach to professional development of higher education faculty. Faculty members were asked to participate in a pre-service technology course. Seventy faculty members accepted the invitation and took the course either during Fall Semester 2001, Winter Semester 2002, or Spring/Summer Terms 2002. Interviews and focus groups were used to determine the impact participation in this technology course had on the faculty members' attitudes toward technology integration in teacher preparation courses as well as their use of technology in their own teacher preparation courses. Our preliminary study found that faculty members are accepting of and will excel in this model of professional development. *[Article copies available for a fee from The Haworth Document Delivery Service: 1-800-HAWORTH. E-mail address: <docdelivery@haworthpress.com> Website: <http://www.HaworthPress.com> © 2004 by The Haworth Press, Inc. All rights reserved.]*

J. AARON POPHAM is Grants and Research Coordinator, Dean's Office, McKay School of Education, Brigham Young University, Provo, UT 84602 (E-mail: aaron_popham@byu.edu).
REBECCA ROCQUE is a graduate student, Department of Instructional Psychology and Technology, Brigham Young University, Provo, UT 84602 (E-mail: rocquere@mstar2.net).

[Haworth co-indexing entry note]: "Faculty-as-Students: Teacher Education Faculty Meaningfully Engaged in a Pre-Service Technology Course." Popham, J. Aaron, and Rebecca Rocque. Co-published simultaneously in *Computers in the Schools* (The Haworth Press, Inc.) Vol. 21, No. 1/2, 2004, pp. 115-126; and: *Integrating Information Technology into the Teacher Education Curriculum: Process and Products of Change* (ed: Nancy Wentworth, Rodney Earle, and Michael L. Connell) The Haworth Press, Inc., 2004, pp. 115-126. Single or multiple copies of this article are available for a fee from The Haworth Document Delivery Service [1-800-HAWORTH, 9:00 a.m. - 5:00 p.m. (EST). E-mail address: docdelivery@haworthpress.com].

KEYWORDS. Professional development, technology integration, technology skill acquisition

This pilot study reports on one component of a larger Preparing Tomorrow's Teachers to Use Technology (PT3) grant project focused on the integration of technology into the teacher education program at Brigham Young University. One goal of the PT3 grant was to help teacher education faculty develop skills in technology use, model the proper use of those skills to pre-service teachers, and implement technology assignments in their courses. Over the past year, as the faculty worked together on committees, participated in workshops or talked informally, the topic of technology integration became a common conversation. Faculty wanted to know what their students knew, what technology skills they had, how to gain these skills themselves, how to change their curriculum to incorporate technology, and how to create meaningful assignments that used technology. Over and over again, the instructors for the Instructional Psychology and Technology (IPT286) course were approached with questions, suggestions, and requests for help. On a whim, one instructor said, "I think everyone should take the technology course along with the students." As we thought about this idea and discussed the possible ramifications, it seemed like a great possibility. With the support of the IPT286 course instructors, the PT3 project directors, and with minor adjustments to the course curriculum, the idea blossomed into a viable plan. As part of their professional development faculty were invited to complete the technology course required for all pre-service teachers. Participants agreed to:

1. Complete course assignments and develop "products" for use in the pre-service courses they teach.
2. Model the use of these "products" in pre-service courses.
3. Create assignments for their students in their pre-service courses during the semesters following their completion of the course that use the skills gained in the technology course.
4. Participate in focus groups to share their experiences in learning and then in using technology in their courses.

The IPT286 course that the faculty agreed to participate in was taught in two different formats. The first format was a one-credit-hour course that followed a self-guided skills acquisition format. The participants, both the faculty and the students, would work through seven major assignment areas on their own time in an open computer lab. Those areas were a lab orientation, introduction to computers, Microsoft Office 2001, telecommunications, HTML coding, HyperStudio, and readings. The assignments were meant for the participants to learn a new skill set and how to integrate that skill set into their day-to-day activities (i.e., lesson plans, Web pages, grade book, etc.).

The second format was a two-credit-hour course that followed a more traditional track. The two-credit-hour course had a weekly one-hour lecture focusing on instructional design and technology integration. The participants had periodic pop quizzes based on previous lecture material as well as assigned readings. Participants were required to maintain a reflective journal and produce a final project. The final project was a major unit plan that incorporated lesson plans, transparencies, a bulletin board sketch, and a HyperStudio stack. There was also a final exam given at the end of the semester. The participants were also required to complete the same self-guided assignment set from the one-credit-hour course.

Faculty participants were encouraged to participate in the two-credit-hour format because it offered the greatest amount of skill acquisition with instructional design and technology integration instruction. They were also encouraged to take the two-credit-hour format because a majority of the faculty involved taught either early childhood and/or elementary education courses and their students were required to take the two-credit-hour course for their major. Secondary education majors were only required to take the one-credit-hour course. Of the 70 participants only 37% agreed to take the two-credit course. Many cited time as the major reason for not investing in the two-credit format. Others felt that the instructional design component of the two-credit-hour course was not necessary for them to receive.

DATA COLLECTION

The data collection for this pilot study was qualitative in nature. Focus group interviews, classroom observations, and examination of course syllabi were used as tools. Comments to PT3 grant leaders from the faculty during the course were reviewed and reported. While the larger study focused on the process of change for the entire teacher education program, this study reports on the faculty who volunteered to complete the technology course required for all pre-service teachers in the current program. The primary research questions included:

1. Is the Faculty-as-Students Model effective for professional development of higher education faculty in a teacher preparation program?
2. Does it promote change in the use of technology in participants' course syllabi and assignments?
3. Is this model more effective than traditional workshops and seminars in helping faculty integrate technology into their courses?

The following is a list of questions developed for the focus group and individual interviews.

Group A: Questions Regarding the Technology Course Curriculum

1. What are your feelings and observations regarding the curriculum in the IPT286 pre-service technology course?
2. What are some of your successes with the content/curriculum?
3. What are some of your failures/frustrations with the content/curriculum?
4. Are the skills taught/gained relevant to the McKay School of Education pre-service teacher preparation program?
5. Are the skills taught/gained relevant to your course(s)?

Group B: Questions Regarding Personal Change

1. How have your ideas/thought processes regarding the use of technology changed due to your experiences in IPT286?
2. Are you or have you changed your teaching and content delivery methods in any way because of your IPT286 experiences?
3. Has being in the same classroom as your students allowed you to better relate to them?
4. Has having the shared IPT286 experience started new conversations between you and your colleagues?
5. Have you worked with other colleagues while completing assignments?
6. Are you discussing curricular and/or program changes?
7. What have you learned together?

Group C: Questions Regarding Curricular Changes

1. Do you feel you can change your curriculum to use the skills/knowledge/understanding you have gained?

2. Are you going to change your curriculum to use the skills/knowledge/understanding you have gained?
3. What are you or have you changed in your curriculum and/or assignments because of your IPT286 experiences?
4. Do you feel you better know what you can expect from your students in their use of technology?

Group D: Questions Regarding Program Changes and the Faculty-as-Students Model

1. Do you see the potential for program changes based on your IPT286 experiences?
2. What kind of program changes would you propose based on your IPT286 experiences?
3. Do you think that the Faculty-as-Students Model taking the technology services course model is a good one?
4. If you participated in last year's traditional workshop training, compare and contrast the differences.
5. Is the Faculty-as-Students Model better? Why?
6. Is the traditional workshop model better? Why?
7. Why do you feel one is better than the other?
8. Which do you feel you learned the most in? Why?
9. Which has had or do you think will have a greater impact on your teaching methods and curriculum?

Group E: Questions Regarding Miscellaneous Ideas

1. What were you hoping to learn? And have you?
2. What were you expecting the course to be like? And did it meet your expectations?
3. What roadblocks have you run up against? What were your greatest successes?
4. What kind of preparation do you recommend for faculty-as-students prior to taking IPT286?

RESULTS

Seventy faculty members agreed to complete the technology course; 28 Fall Semester 2001, 24 Winter Semester 2002, 8 Spring/Summer Terms 2002, and 10 Fall Semester 2002. Seven percent of the faculty members who enrolled in Fall Semester 2001 dropped from the program; one left the faculty and returned to the K-12 arena full-time and the second was retiring in a year and felt the work was not worth his time. Sixty-one percent of the faculty members who enrolled in Fall Semester 2001 completed the course, with 25-30% completing the assignment on time. Thirty-two percent of the faculty felt a time crunch and spread the course over the duration of both Fall Semester 2001 and Winter Semester 2002. Of the 32% who tried to spread the course over two semesters, 9% did not finish the course. The one professor who didn't finish received additional assignments from the department and expanded an experimental electronic portfolio assignment in his course that demanded a great deal of his time. This meant that 89% of those who started the course work during Fall Semester 2001 eventually finished the work successfully.

Fall Semester 2001 showed some of the best results. The early adopters and most committed faculty participated during Fall Semester 2001. Of those who started the IPT286 course in Winter Semester 2002, only 50% finished the course work. Of the 50% who did not finish the course work, 42% were junior faculty who were greatly concerned about their tenure and felt that taking the course was distracting them from their research and writing. They dropped from the course to focus on tenure. One participant was on a temporary contract and left campus, one became extremely ill, and one received a whole new set of assignments from the dean that demanded all of the participant's time. One other participant caught the vision of using BlackBoard as an instructional tool and did not finish the course because she started completely restructuring her course and moving it onto BlackBoard. This intense restructuring of her course took most of her time, keeping her from completing the course work. Twenty-five percent of the participants simply did not have the time and abandoned the process.

Spring/summer terms were the least successful. Only 13% of the participants finished the course work (one of eight). Thirty-eight percent of the participants were junior faculty, who, like their predecessors, were highly concerned with their tenure and felt they could not finish the course work due to the distractions it held. Fifty percent of the participants simply abandoned the process.

Fall Semester 2002 showed our greatest results but only slightly better than Fall Semester 2001. Ninety percent (nine out of ten) of those who started the course work finished. The one participant who did not finish was a junior faculty concerned with tenure.

From the interviews and focus groups it was found that 64% of the faculty felt that the course should be spread over a period of two semesters for faculty. The course work was too demanding with their existing teaching and research responsibilities. The faculty members suggested that having an optional weekly seminar would be helpful. This would allow them to meet with the course instructor or a teaching assistant to ask questions and get additional help with assignments. This would also create an atmosphere of communication and collaboration with the group. A natural peer lead support system would also be created.

Results of the Focus Group and Individual Interviews

Twenty-two of the 28 faculty members enrolled in Fall Semester 2001 participated in an interview or focus group. One faculty member missed her focus group, the two that dropped opted not to participate, and the last three didn't have enough of an experience to warrant comment.

Group A. From this group of questions the focus was on questions four and five that concentrated on the relevance of the technology course curriculum to the pre-service preparation program and the faculty member's course in general. The feeling was that the course has great relevance as a whole. There was concern regarding two of the modules, HTML coding and HyperStudio. Many faculty members didn't feel there was any relevance for HTML coding to their courses in particular. Of the 22 interviewed 17 struggled with the HTML module to the point of wanting to give up the project. On the other hand, all 22 found the Microsoft Office module extremely relevant, most particularly PowerPoint.

Group B. Questions one and two concentrated on the changes in individual faculty members' thought processes regarding the use of technology and their teaching methods. It was found that most of the faculty had already begun to rethink their uses of technology in their courses prior to this experience. However, participation in this course solidified their resolve to make changes to their own courses. It also gave them the confidence and the needed technology skills to make the desired changes. Sixteen of the 22 added or expanded the use of PowerPoint in their course, either for personal use or as assignments for their students. The entire group has begun to use some type of electronic communication with their colleagues and/or students.

Group C. The primary focus in this group of questions was whether or not the faculty members better understood the knowledge and skills their students brought to their courses. The interview indicated a re-sounding yes. All of the faculty felt they could hold their students to a higher standard and ask more of them with regard to technology use and integration. They felt they could include more technology requirements in various assignments. Many did not feel that they would change their present curriculum significantly to better take advantage of their new-found skills nor the skills the students bring to the table.

Group D. This group of questions received a lot of time in the inter-views and focus groups and was thoroughly explored. Twenty of the 22 felt participation in the pre-service technology course was an excellent form of professional development. Overall, this was an extremely posi-tive experience for the faculty with very few frustrations.

The faculty members were asked to compare this experience with other traditional workshops/seminars they had participated in. They felt that the traditional model (workshop/seminars) heightened their aware-ness of available technologies and possible uses but didn't allow them the time to learn the skills needed to incorporate the use of these prod-ucts into their courses. Many times following a traditional work-shop/seminar, they felt frustrated as they returned to their offices to try and use what they had seen. For most, they could not make the technol-ogy work as they had seen it demonstrated. Many of them abandoned trying to use technology because they did not have the time or the pa-tience to figure it out.

The faculty found participation in the pre-service technology course a wonderful experience because they could learn at their own pace with the guided tutorials and help from computer lab assistants. The tutorials gave them something to refer back to and they had constant teaching as-sistant help when questions or problems arose. They have been able to generalize the skills gained to their everyday lives. One faculty member learned how to use several software packages that he had at home and had no idea previously how to use them. Learning how to use them made him extremely happy. The faculty member had bought the com-puter so he could work from home but was unable to use the technology; now he has the skills and confidence to succeed.

Group E. This group of questions concentrated on the learning de-sires of the participants and whether or not they were met. The first and foremost goal of all the faculty members was to better understand the technology skills their students would bring to their course. They wanted to know if they could make changes to their courses and if the students could meet the expectations of those changes. They all ex-pressed that they now know what to expect from their students. They can now say, "I know what is taught in the technology course and you can do this assignment." Some felt that they could make many small changes to assignments because they know their students should be able to do the work. From there the learning desires greatly deviated by individual. PowerPoint was the most desirable technology skill. The PowerPoint module gave them a basic knowledge, but some felt they needed more advanced applications to better use this tool. The greatest disappointment came for those seeking Web design skills. Many felt the HTML coding module was too difficult and had no relevance because there are so many Web editors available for use.

Comments from Faculty Regarding the IPT286 Course

Following are comments made to the PT3 project director(s) and/or IPT286 class instructors as e-mail messages:

- The class has been very interesting and beneficial for me. (I have substituted many of the lab assignments to meet my personal interests and needs–but the lab assistants have no way of signing off on these–any suggestions?) Yes, it is difficult to be a student again especially meeting deadlines. (I haven't done so well here–certainly I wouldn't get an "A"!)
- I've been grateful for the accommodations Becky [the instructor] has made for us. She's allowed us to put HyperStudio on our laptops, which will be a great blessing as we're off campus for four weeks during the time those assignments are due. The lab aides have been very polite in my experience with them.
- Thanks for helping set this up for the faculty. (I think it would be helpful if the deadlines could be adjusted for faculty–possibly extending through two semesters rather than one. I know Roger has felt overwhelmed, but would be able to succeed if the time constraints weren't a factor.)
- I'm slowly making progress–I just need time, doesn't everyone? I heard we could have HyperStudio put on our laptop–so we can work at home. Who do I talk to about that?
- I have learned a bunch and want to finish up Winter. I would like to learn all that the course has to offer. I will be in touch with you after the first of the year. Thanks for the opportunity.
- Enjoyed the class on Wednesday. The timeline was great. The first assignments are helpful. I look forward to the rest.

- Thank you for your wonderful class. I have loved learning from you. I feel like you have become my treasured and respected friend. I can't believe how much I have learned in such a short time.
- I have some concerns about being able to finish this in one semester. Is it possible to extend it through next semester or do I need to just suck up and finish it this semester?
- Well, I will tell you that I've decided not to do the class. From the packet and zip that was given to me, it seems that the information is presented for Apple/Mac, but I am a PC person, so I'm not doing the assignments. I admit that I did not take the time to find out if the assignments were also written for PC platforms. The reason I didn't do this was most of the things that were part of the syllabus I already know how to do–I am very competent with word processing, clip art, word art, tables, formatting, etc.; I can use spreadsheets and databases, I can merge; I use PowerPoint for every class I teach; I've scanned documents; my family Christmas newsletter includes multiple columns, photos, clip art, calendar, etc.; so, I'm pretty technologically with it. I was hoping to learn about video editing and HTML–but not with a Mac. So, again, it might sound like I am whining and complaining–and in fact I might be. But the course is not going so well for me.

After receiving the last e-mail above, a project member sat down with the faculty member and discussed her concerns. She was about to be the first dropout. The project member, with permission from the course instructor, restructured the assignments to better meet the needs of the faculty member. She was shown how to use the existing tutorials and class materials with her PC technology, which completely changed her outlook. The faculty member focused on HTML and video editing. She started to produce her own class Web site, which took advantage of effective teaching videos she produced with her video-editing skills.

CONCLUSION

We have found in this pilot study that the faculty-as-students taking the technology service course model is an effective form of professional development for higher education faculty in a teacher preparation program. The faculty has found that they have been able to better learn the technology skills presented to them and that they have found ways to better generalize those skills to their own courses and research. The traditional conference/workshop model opened their eyes to possible uses of technology, while the Faculty-as-Students Model gave them the skills needed to produce technology-enhanced products, model those products, and write meaningful assignments for their students. Twenty of the 22 participants in focus group and individual interviews recommended the continual use of this model and would recommend the model for use at other institutions of higher learning. One of the most valuable outcomes of this project has been the open communication between faculty members across several departments. As they have worked on assignments together and met with the course instructors, students, and each other, many barriers have been removed and they look forward to a continuation of learning and working together. The IPT286 course instructors as well as the director of the Teaching and Learning Support Center and teaching assistants are more open to faculty suggestions and the faculty are more willing to try new technology in their own courses. More time will be needed to measure the extent of the impact this experience will have on the faculty members as they continue to revise their curriculum and assignments to include technology. Some of the pros of the Faculty-as-Students Model follow:

1. The faculty gained a new set of skills in using technology and confidence in modeling its use with their students.
2. The two-credit-hour participants gained a greater understanding and appreciation for the power of technology.
3. The IPT286 course is self-paced with support.
4. The experience opened up communication across the college and partnership schools and increased the willingness to collaborate and take risks.

Though there were a great deal of positives as a result of this experience and the faculty would overwhelmingly recommend this form of professional development, there were some cons, which follow:

1. The time commitment to successfully complete the course work was too great for many faculty.
2. The course tutorials and assignments were designed for use on the Macintosh platform only.
3. The faculty members were at multiple levels of skills, needs, and interest.
4. There was a large demand on course and lab resources for preparation and course delivery to the faculty versus students.
5. The rollover in graduate instructors with little background in instructional design or public education was too high.

One of the greatest outcomes of this experience was the knowledge that the IPT286 technology course was outdated and needed to focus less on skills acquisition, though important, and more on good instructional design and the seamless integration of technology into instruction and lesson plan preparation. The positive response to the Faculty-as-Students Model shows the need for further research in this area and further development of this model for faculty development. To do so would mean that the IPT286 course at this institution and similar courses at other institutions would need to be reevaluated and focus on the acquisition of good instructional design and technology integration skills versus skills acquisition. This was one of the recommendations made to the instructors of the IPT286 course. This pilot study shows that existing higher education courses can be used as a form of professional development for higher education faculty. Further studies should be done to see if a restructured technology course focusing on instructional design instead of skills acquisition would be as successful with the Faculty-as-Students Model as it has been with this skill-acquisition-based format.

Charles Graham
Richard Culatta
Mitchell Pratt
Richard West

Redesigning the Teacher Education Technology Course to Emphasize Integration

SUMMARY. Teacher education programs in the United States are trying to equip tomorrow's teachers with the technology skills needed to impact learning in the classroom. During the past decade there has been a realization that teaching technology skills alone is not adequate–pre-service teachers must also learn how to integrate the use of technology into their curriculum. This paper describes BYU's instructional technology course and the design process that a team of instructors went through to redesign the course in order to put greater emphasis on technology integration. An iterative redesign approach was used. Several

CHARLES GRAHAM is Assistant Professor, Department of Instructional Psychology and Technology, Brigham Young University, Provo, UT 84602 (E-mail: Charles_graham@byu.edu).
RICHARD CULATTA is a graduate student, Department of Instructional Psychology and Technology, Brigham Young University, Provo, UT 84602 (E-mail: culatta@byu.edu).
MITCHELL PRATT is Adjunct Professor, Department of Instructional Psychology and Technology, Brigham Young University, Provo, UT 84602 (E-mail: mitch_pratt@byu.edu).
RICHARD WEST is a graduate student, Department of Instructional Psychology and Technology, Brigham Young University, Provo, UT 84602 (E-mail: rick_west1@yahoo.com).

[Haworth co-indexing entry note]: "Redesigning the Teacher Education Technology Course to Emphasize Integration." Graham, Charles et al. Co-published simultaneously in *Computers in the Schools* (The Haworth Press, Inc.) Vol. 21, No. 1/2, 2004, pp. 127-148; and: *Integrating Information Technology into the Teacher Education Curriculum: Process and Products of Change* (ed: Nancy Wentworth, Rodney Earle, and Michael L. Connell) The Haworth Press, Inc., 2004, pp. 127-148. Single or multiple copies of this article are available for a fee from The Haworth Document Delivery Service [1-800-HAWORTH, 9:00 a.m. - 5:00 p.m. (EST). E-mail address: docdelivery@haworthpress.com].

Digital Object Identifier: 10.1300/J025v21n01_10

127

iterations of the course redesign will be shared along with the strengths and limitations discovered in the design and implementation process. *[Article copies available for a fee from The Haworth Document Delivery Service: 1-800-HAWORTH. E-mail address: <docdelivery@haworthpress.com> Website: <http://www.HaworthPress.com> © 2004 by The Haworth Press, Inc. All rights reserved.]*

KEYWORDS. Technology integration, technology skills, teacher education, technology instruction

INTRODUCTION

The past decade has brought with it sweeping changes in access to technology in the classroom (National Center for Educational Statistics, 2003). Current trends indicate that the availability of technology in the classroom is outpacing the number of teachers who know how to effectively teach with the technology. In 1999 a national survey showed that only 20% of teachers felt well prepared to integrate technology into their teaching (National Center for Educational Statistics, 1999b). At that same time 51% of public school classrooms had Internet access and the ratio of students to instructional computers was 6:1 (National Center for Educational Statistics, 1999a). Since that time the availability of computers in classrooms has increased dramatically. With 99% of public schools in the United States reporting access to the Internet, the ratio of students to instructional computers with Internet access has decreased to 4.8:1. In addition, the number of instructional rooms in public schools with Internet access has risen to 92% (National Center for Educational Statistics, 2003). This increase in classroom technology availability shifts the emphasis for effectively integrating technology from the hardware to the teacher. This is a positive trend because simply providing useful hardware does not equate to successful technology integration (Thornburg, 2003).

Two primary barriers to effective use of information technology (IT) in the classroom are (a) a lack of confidence with technology skills and (b) a lack of knowledge regarding how to integrate technology into the curriculum (Hargrave & Hsu, 2000). In 1996 Willis and Mehlinger reported that few programs were actively investigating how to incorporate technology instruction into methods courses and field experiences (Willis, 1996). This finding was reiterated by an ISTE study that reported most student teachers do not use technology in their field experiences even though technology is available in most of their classrooms (Moursund & Bielfeldt, 1999). The primary source of IT instruction in teacher preparation programs is traditionally a single required instructional technology course that focuses on computer literacy rather than technology integration.

Increased awareness of the need to emphasize technology integration in teacher preparation programs is occurring due to programs such as the Preparing Tomorrow's Teachers to Use Technology (PT3) grants. Hargrave and Hsu (2000), in their survey of 88 higher education programs, found that although a single IT course is still the predominant way of teaching technology, there is an increasing move from teaching productivity skills toward curriculum integration of technology (Hargrave & Hsu, 2000). BYU's PT3 grant has been a force supporting change in both the instructional technology course as well as in methods courses. This paper will document the story and process behind the changes that have occurred in BYU's instructional technology course as it was redesigned to have a greater focus on technology integration.

BACKGROUND AND CONTEXT

BYU's teacher education program licenses about 1,000 graduating students each year. The majority of these students are required to take an instructional technology course (IPT286) offered through the Instructional Psychology & Technology Department (IP&T). Elementary education students are required to take a two-credit-hour version of the course and secondary education students, who are distributed throughout the different Arts and Sciences Colleges, are required to take a one-credit-hour version of the course. Elementary education students are required to take the course early in their program while secondary education students have the liberty to take the course at any time–which often leads them to take it toward the end of their programs of study.

The Challenge

In August 2002 Graham was given the assignment to coordinate several sections of IPT286 being taught by faculty, adjunct faculty, and graduate students. As part of his academic assignment, he was also asked to take a critical look at the course to determine what changes, if any, should be made to improve its value to the pre-service students. The other authors of this paper participated actively in this challenge to analyze and redesign the IPT286 course. Pratt, an adjunct faculty member with 27 years of elementary teaching experience, was concurrently working in a local elementary school. Culatta, a part-time instructor, began teaching technology integration to faculty at the University of Rhode Island, and recently presented at several national and international conferences. West, a graduate student instructor, has been involved in the redesign process. Together (and with the input from many others) we collaborated on the challenge of analyzing and making recommendations for the redesign of BYU's instructional technology course. The body of this paper will describe our struggles and accomplishments in the redesign process.

REDESIGN PROCESS OVERVIEW

Assumptions

We began with the common belief that there was a difference between learning *technology skills* and learning how to *integrate technology* into the classroom. We were unified in the belief that ultimately the integration skills were key to making technology a useful teaching tool. We also acknowledged that, without some basic technology skills, integration was not possible. We agreed that ultimately the job of teaching technology integration was not a task that could be done in a single one- or two-credit course alone. Rather we felt that technology integration was something that needed to be taught and modeled across our own teacher education curriculum.

Stages

Although it seemed like the discipline-specific methods courses would be the ideal context for students to be learning technology integration skills, the pragmatic barriers to achieving that end seemed insurmountable on a reasonable timetable. Some of the most daunting barriers are described in Table 1.

These barriers make impractical a single jump from the current to the ideal condition of having instructors of all the methods courses embrace teaching and modeling technology integration. The IPT286 course is a service course designed to support students and faculty in the teacher

TABLE 1. Barriers to Redesigning Curriculum to Teach Integration Only in Methods Courses

Barrier	Description
Incoming Student Technology Skill Level	Merrill, a BYU IP&T faculty member, did a study looking at the technology skills of students enrolling in the IPT286 course (Merrill, 2003). He found that, while the majority of students had experience with word processing, e-mail, and Internet browsing, most did not have substantial experience with other applications commonly used to integrate technology into the classroom such as spreadsheets, Web page design tools, multimedia, etc. A small number of students do not have even basic computer literacy comprehension such as electronic file types and management. With limited time for instruction, less can be taught about integration when more time must be spent teaching technology skills.
Faculty Technology Skill Level	Like students, faculty members also have a diverse range of technology skills and many do not feel comfortable teaching technology applications to students. Also, methods faculty do not often want to take time away from their established curriculum to teach technology skills to students who do not have those skills.
Curriculum Change Difficulty	Moving from a single information technology course to teaching technology integration in the methods courses requires gathering support from many people, which takes time. Making changes to the curriculum is very time consuming. At BYU there is an approval process that can take up to a year and require approval from teacher education as well as the 31 arts and sciences disciplines across campus that have teacher preparation majors.

education program. In this role the course can act as a catalyst for progress by providing a basic level of technology integration skill development for students as methods faculty increase their use of technology in their own courses. Figure 1 shows a timeline depicting the changing role of the instructional technology course. The top half of the figure represents instruction that focuses on technology skills while the bottom half of the figure represents instruction that focuses on integration. Time is represented in the figure moving from left to right along the diagonal line.

FIGURE 1. How technology skills and integration are taught at BYU in the past, present, and future.

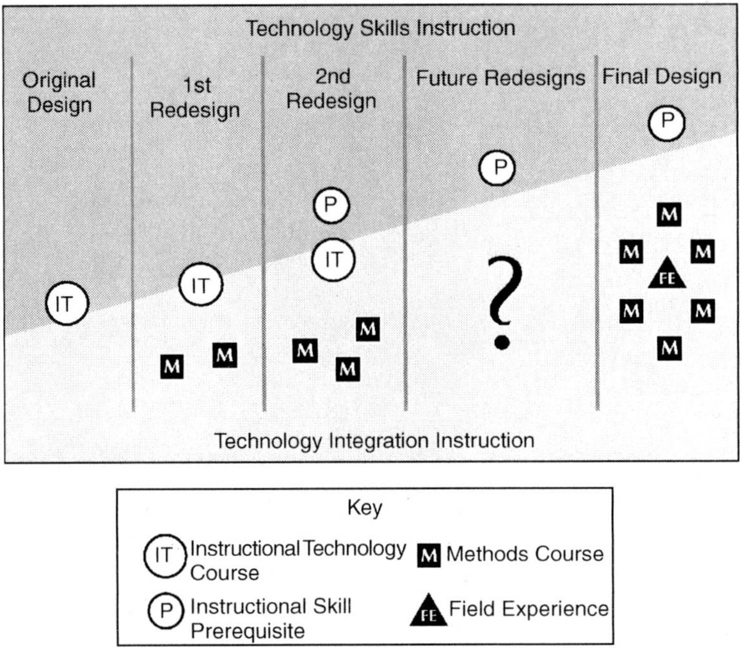

The stage represented in the leftmost column of the figure represents a simplified view of how technology skills and integration were initially taught in the BYU School of Education. The stage represented in the rightmost column of the figure represents a vision for how technology skills and integration might be taught at some point in the future. An important aspect to note is the move over time to emphasize instruction that focuses on integration rather than skills in the instructional technology course. Additionally, it is important to note the increasing numbers of methods courses over time that begin to model how to use technology in the classroom. This paper will detail the specific changes to the IPT286 course and outline the process that has allowed the changes to occur.

The body of this paper will describe two iterations in the evolving design of the IPT286 course at BYU. We hope to express a realistic sense of the barriers and challenges faced as well as successes and lessons learned in the process. We will begin by briefly describing the initial state of the course before the redesign (see Original Design in Figure 1). At this time the course had a strong focus on technology skills that would promote teacher productivity. Secondly, we will describe the first design, which attempted to teach both basic technology skills and integration skills (see column labeled 1st Redesign in Figure 1). Thirdly, we will describe the design iteration currently underway that will create a basic technology skill prerequisite for the course and free up time and resources to focus more on the integration aspects of the course. Finally, we will speculate on future challenges and ideas for possible design iterations which may help move us toward our goals.

IPT286 ORIGINAL DESIGN

The Design

The original design of the technology course consisted of three parts: (a) a hands-on technology lab, (b) readings from a textbook, and (c) a weekly one-hour lecture. Secondary education students enrolled in IPT286 for only one credit hour were not required to attend the weekly lecture. Participation in the three portions of the course combined to give the student a final grade. As Figure 2 shows, the lecture portion of the course was intended to focus on technology integration, while the hands-on portion was intended to focus on technology skills. The reading portion was intended to blend technology skills and technology integration.

While Figure 2 shows the even balance between the different parts intended by the original design of the course, this balance was not perceived by the students. This was in part due to the breakdown of the course assignments as shown in Figure 3.

In addition to the greater weight of the technology skills final grade, the lecture grade did not require active participation. If students showed up for class, he/she would receive the full grade for the lecture portion, regardless of participation. This shifts the balance even further toward the side of technology skills instruction. During the last few semesters of the original course design, quizzes were added at the beginning of the lecture section in an attempt to improve student participation. The following sections will describe in detail the three portions of the course.

Weekly lecture. Each week the elementary education students attended a one-hour lecture held in a large lecture hall. Large sections (av-

FIGURE 2. The breakdown of the original IT course was designed to provide balance between technology integration instruction and technology skills training.

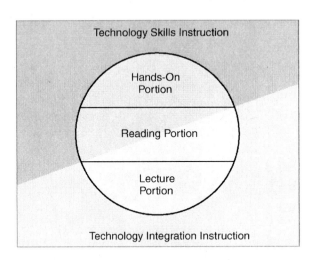

FIGURE 3. Grading in the IT course was weighted more toward technology skills than integration.

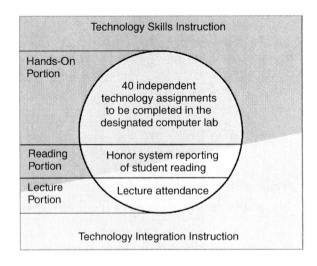

eraging over 100 students each semester) and lack of student access to technology in the room led to traditional lecture-style teaching, with the instructor presenting information and students taking notes. Interaction between students and instructor was also limited due to the high student-to-teacher ratio. The weekly lectures were designed to provide students with a conceptual framework and background for technology use in the classroom. Lecture topics were centered on student learning methods, technology integration methods, and instructional design principles. In general, however, the emphasis of the lecture portion of the course was based on instructional design theory. While the lectures provided a very detailed view of methodology and design principles, they did not include any practical applications of the methodology or how the principles might be applied in the classroom.

Textbook readings. The reading portion of the course was intended to provide the students with additional technology integration and design information that was not included in the lectures. In addition, the textbook aimed to blend the technology skills and the technology integration portions of the course (as shown in Figure 2). Much like the lecture topics, the textbook focused on theoretical cases of technology integration or integration principles. Each week students were expected to complete lengthy reading assignments from the text. A portion of a student's final grade was determined by successful completion of these reading assignments. At the end of the semester, students told the instructor which of the reading assignments they had completed. While the topics from the text were similar to those from the lectures, they were rarely arranged to occur at the same time. This lessened the possibility for discussion or application of the reading assignments in the lecture section.

Hands-on technology lab. Since the lecture section and the individual reading portions of the course did not provide the students with the opportunity to use technology, the "hands-on" portion was designed to give students a practical application of the topics from the text and lectures. Because of the high class enrollment, the hands-on portion of the course was completed in an independent study format. At the beginning of the semester, students were given a "Computer Tutorial" book that included all of the assignments for the semester. Assignments were designed to teach one software program at a time. These software titles included Microsoft Office, Macintosh OS, HyperStudio, Netscape Navigator, and iMovie. Each assignment showed students an example of a finished product, such as a newsletter or a spreadsheet. The students then followed a list of steps that led them to complete the product. Upon completion of the steps, a lab assistant would review the product. If the product was identical to the example, they would "pass off" the assignment and could begin working on the next. Once students had successfully "passed off" all of their assignments, they were finished with the hands-on portion of the course.

Strengths of the Design

The primary strength of the original design was that it allowed a small number of faculty members to teach a very large number of students. Since the instructors were not responsible for grading the students (other than taking attendance at the lectures), and did not need to be present for the hands-on portion of the course, it was possible for one instructor to teach upward of 300 students.

Another strength perceived by the students was the assignments in the hands-on portion. Students enjoyed the self-paced nature of that portion of the course. Since the secondary education students were not required to attend the lecture at all, they could be completely finished with the course in just a couple of weeks. In addition, since students were only required to recreate the examples and were provided with step-by-step instructions, it was very easy for students to complete the assignments. This focus on step-by-step instructions allowed students with little prior technology experience to easily complete the assignments.

Limitations of the Design

While the "hands-on" assignments were easy to complete, several problems arose. First, since students were working at their own pace, it was impossible to correlate their assignments with the topics of the lecture section or the readings. Second, since the students followed step-by-step instructions, they did not learn to be problem-solvers with the technology. They relied too heavily on the tutorials. If the tutorial did not tell them exactly what to do, many would become frustrated and unable to complete the task. This problem became apparent one semester when a newer version of Netscape Navigator was loaded onto the machines in the computer lab, and the "Computer Tutorial" book was not updated. Even though the functionality of Netscape required for the completion of the assignment had not changed, the icons in the newer version appeared in 3D and with slightly different colors. Since the icons in the new version of the software did not exactly match those in their tutorial, many students had difficulties completing the assignment. We felt that this was evidence that the tutorial strategy used in the course was teaching students to carefully follow instructions rather than helping them to solve problems with the technology tools. Additionally, developing and maintaining tutorials required tedious revisions almost every semester in order to maintain consistency with the lab software.

Another major limitation to the original design was the lack of technology use in the other portions of the course. Due to the size and location of the lectures, it was impossible for students to be using technology. Ironically, technology was rarely, if ever, used by the instructors of the lecture portion. Not surprisingly, end-of-semester reviews showed that students did not feel that the material being taught was relevant to what they would be expected to do as teachers. One student said, "I just felt that a lot of the things we discussed during actual class time did not necessarily benefit me . . . the lecture information didn't always seem necessary." Students were also frustrated with the amount of reading required for a one- or two-credit course. Many students felt as though the readings in the text were "a lot of busy work."

Another source of frustration for students was the inherent problem of correlating the different portions of the course. Statements such as, "I did not understand the relationship between the lecture part and lab part," were common among the students. Within the original design of the course, this lack of correlation was unavoidable due to the fact that two portions of the course were self-paced.

IPT286 FIRST REDESIGN

In this section we will talk about the first redesign attempt of the IPT286 course. Based on our analysis of the original design as well as on input from the School of Education, we made design changes based on the goals listed in Table 2.

Based on these broad goals, we redesigned the course to try to teach technology skills in the context of learning about technology integration. While we would have preferred to focus much more on integration, inadequate incoming technology literacy levels of many students made it essential to first teach basic technology skills. Figure 4 depicts this shared focus by having the IPT286 course evenly divided between teaching technology skills and teaching integration. A key element preventing us from adequately addressing our goals was the large class size and the lack of technology resources for students in the lecture hall. The

TABLE 2. Overarching Goals for the Instructional Technology Course Redesign

Goal	Rationale
To introduce electronic portfolios	Two primary factors motivated the inclusion of electronic portfolios in IPT286: (a) the School of Education planned to use portfolios as evidence for their NCATE accreditation review and (b) the State of Utah recently passed a law requiring Utah teachers to complete a portfolio as part of their level 2 licensure.
To have a strong focus on integration	Our survey of students and recent graduates regarding their use of technology showed that they used technology primarily for productivity purposes (Mitchell & Graham, 2003). We felt this use pattern was directly linked to how they were taught to use technology in their IPT286 and other education courses. We felt that integration needed to be a focus if our goal was to help teachers begin thinking about using technology in their teaching.
To teach basic technology skills	Despite the desire to focus on technology integration in the class, there are a significant number of students each semester who do not enter with basic technology skills. Because there is no official technology prerequisite for the course, we still needed to teach basic technology skills.
To model technology integration	We felt that it would be hypocritical to teach technology integration without integrating technology into our own teaching. Additionally, we felt that by integrating technology into our own teaching, the students would pick up on tacit aspects of technology integration that cannot be conveyed in a textbook or lecture.

department agreed to our proposed changes, allowing us to reduce the maximum class size from 183 to 50 and to hold the class in a room with computer resources for the students to use. Both two- and one-credit versions of the section began meeting weekly. During the semester students were also assigned to learning teams so that they could benefit from one another's support and creativity.

The Design

The activities in the redesigned course fall into three major categories: (a) activities related to standards and e-portfolios, (b) activities related to teacher productivity, and (c) activities related to modeling technology integration. Each of these three areas had elements of both technology skills instruction as well as technology integration instruction, as can be seen in Figure 4. The remainder of this section describes each of these areas in greater detail.

Standards and electronic portfolios. Although paper portfolios had been required in several teacher education classes, the use and creation of electronic portfolios were a fairly new phenomenon being explored both at the school and state level. The PT3 grant provided financial support for Graham to participate in two professional conferences in order to learn more about portfolios and strategies for introducing the concept of e-portfolios to students in the IPT286 course. These experiences, along with connections established through PT3 networks, allowed Graham to learn from national leaders such as Helen Barrett as well as to collaborate with state and local district leaders to develop a vision for how electronic portfolios might transition seamlessly when students move from pre-service to in-service status (Graham, Webb, Hawkins, & Harlan, 2003).

The initial impetus for the Teacher Education Department wanting electronic portfolios to be introduced in IPT286 was that other instructors were concerned about the technological skills that it might require. We have found that the technology aspect of the portfolio is easy to learn compared to other more conceptual issues that must be learned, such as understanding the INTASC teaching standards, selecting artifacts, and creating quality reflections. Introducing the e-portfolio in the IPT286 course has added a lot of new content to the course without adding additional time or resources to address it.

FIGURE 4. IT course redesign focuses both on teaching technology skills *and* integration, with the goal of moving toward technology integration.

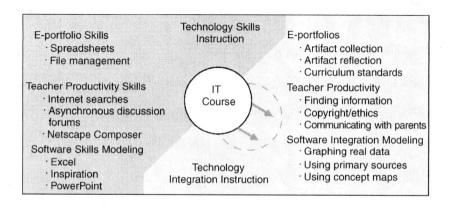

Tools for teacher productivity. The second category of course activities concerns using technology to improve teacher productivity. Students learn about the state core curriculum standards and where to find them online. They are then exposed to many of the online tools and databases of teacher resources available through the Utah Educational Network. They are taught Internet searching skills and how to assess the credibility of online resources they find. They are also required to use the Internet to find specific resources to help them teach a selected core curriculum standard. Secondly, the pre-service teachers learn how to compose and upload Web pages in the context of creating a Web site to communicate with parents of their students. The pre-service students learn the rules of copyright and fair use and apply those rules to the images and media elements that they use in creating their parent Web site and throughout the rest of the semester.

Modeling Sessions and Technology Integration

Attending the Society for Information Technology and Teacher Education (SITE) conference had a significant impact on the redesign of the IPT286 course. One of the important ideas discussed in a conference keynote address was the importance of K-12 students using technology instead of the instructor being the primary user of technology. Additionally a group of presenters from Arizona State University shared their successful practice of having pre-service students involved in a modeling session followed by a debriefing session where the class as a collective group could reflect on how technology was used in the session. This provided some impetus for developing a series of modeling sessions where we as instructors would use technology to teach a K-12 lesson with our students taking on the role of the K-12 students. We developed this series of modeling sessions in three general content areas. Secondary students who are taking the course for one credit participate in only one modeling session (the one most closely related to their major) while the elementary education majors participate in all three modeling and debriefing sessions. Table 3 provides a brief summary of these sessions.

Strengths of the Design

Aspects of the redesign were implemented for the first time in the winter 2003 semester, with the full implementation, including the modeling sessions, being taught for the first time during the summer 2003 terms. We have been pleased with many of the outcomes of the course

TABLE 3. Description of Three Modeling Sessions Taught in IPT286

Content Area (Technology Used and Taught)	Description
Math/Science (Excel spreadsheets, PowerPoint)	In the math/science modeling session, students conduct an experiment where they build balloon rockets (balloons attached to straws). Different student teams have balloons of different diameters, and they measure the distances the balloons travel. All of this data is entered into a spreadsheet and graphed. Then the teams put together a presentation for the class describing the experiment, hypothesis, data, findings, etc.
Social Studies (Inspiration, PowerPoint)	The social studies modeling lesson focuses on finding and using primary source materials available online to create a multimedia presentation on a particular topic in the core curriculum (some sections focus on the civil rights movement and others, Utah pioneers). Students create a concept map using Inspiration to link people and events in the planning of their projects. They then use the Internet to find primary source materials to enrich their multimedia presentations.
Language Arts (Inspiration, PowerPoint)	The language arts modeling session focuses on the use of concept mapping tools to help students prepare to write and animate a rhyme book. Students begin by reading a traditional rhyme book. They then are given some suffixes such as "-all" or "-ight" and they begin to use Inspiration to brainstorm all the words that match their suffixes. From the words that are generated, teams develop a story that rhymes. This story is put into PowerPoint and animated using images and sounds. (Secondary education students do a different modeling session where they map the structure of a narrative and an expository text.)

redesign. One of our instructors received the following e-mail from a colleague:

> In the past students were all grumbling about what an incredible waste of time it was [IPT286], that it was fluff, that it was not applicable, etc. The students who are in it now are extremely happy. I was recently reviewing a lesson plan with a girl and commented on the professionalism of her presentation. She said she owed it all to the class. Several others piped up in unison that it was an excellent class–not at all like the rumors they heard.

Students particularly seem to enjoy the modeling sessions; we have had comments from students about how "fun" the learning in these sessions is. We have also observed the students' active engagement during these sessions. Even though students who take the IPT286 course typically have very little experience, if any, with teaching or preparing lessons, they leave the course being able to talk about specific ways technology might be used in the classroom.

Limitations of the Design

While it is encouraging for the instructors to see many of the students engaged and excited about what they are learning in the class, the changes have not been a panacea, and we are aware of many limitations of the redesign. The greatest limitation is that for many of the students with low incoming technology skills, the course attempts to cover too much ground in too little time–everything in the course is new to them. For example, many do not know what a lesson plan is, most have never heard of electronic portfolios, and teaching standards, such as INTASC, are new. This attempt to focus on integration and to have the students simultaneously acquire basic technology skills has led to cognitive overload, particularly for students with low entry technology skill levels. Students with moderate-to-high technology skill levels seem to perform without problems. One aspect of the course that quickly became apparent to every IPT286 teacher was that there was an incredible spread between high-achieving, "technology-wise" students and struggling "computer-illiterate" students. Because the elementary education program attracts students who want to work with children, and not necessarily computers, there are typically more students at the low end than the upper end of the spectrum. This presents a dilemma to the course instructors: At what basic skill level do they teach the course? Invariably there are students who feel like the pace of instruction is much too slow and others who feel overwhelmed.

An additional challenge is managing student expectations for the course. There are many students each semester who start with the expectation that an instructional technology course is going to primarily teach technology skills. These students are sometimes frustrated that they are being asked to apply the skills at the same time that they are learning the technology skills. Others enter with the expectation from previous semesters that if they are already technology literate, this course will be an "easy A" and require minimal time from their schedules.

A final limitation we will mention in this paper has to do with the fact that our modeling sessions take place in a very technology-rich environment where the student-to-computer ratio is very low. We realize that many of the students will not end up teaching under these same conditions. It would be nice to have modeling sessions that varied the computing resources available so that students could experience methods that work in the "one-computer classroom" as well as the computer lab environment.

IPT286 SECOND REDESIGN

The Proposed Design

There are three basic features that we propose will impact the next version of the course redesign. We hope that these will address the major limitations of the current course design. These three basic features are (a) adding a basic technology skills prerequisite for the course, (b) requesting a curriculum change requiring secondary education majors to take the course for two credits instead of one, and (c) introducing students to program portfolio concepts before taking the course. Implementation of the technology prerequisite will allow the IPT286 course to focus more intently on integration ideas and skills as shown in Figure 5. It will also free up some time to teach other technology skills important to the faculty such as how to use scanners, digital cameras, and video-editing software. This section will describe the details of each of these features.

Technology Skills Prerequisite

The key change will be the addition of a technology skills prerequisite for the IPT286 course. This seemed to be the most logical solution to the current problem, and we felt that this would be an acceptable solution for many reasons. First, it is not unprecedented because other schools have implemented similar prerequisites. Second, technology standards for K-12 students, as specified in the ISTE NETS-S standards and the new Utah core curriculum standards will likely indicate that increasingly future incoming students should have basic technology skills. Having a technology skills prerequisite for the course would eliminate many of the challenges associated with the current design, like the divide between the technologically savvy and technologically

FIGURE 5. The plan to implement a technology prerequisite to cover basic technology skills instruction.

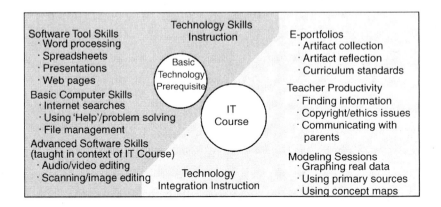

illiterate students. A prerequisite would allow students with a technology deficit to acquire remediation on their own time frame while not holding back those students who are better prepared. Important aspects of adding a prerequisite are (a) a mechanism for assessing whether a student meets the prerequisite or not and (b) resources for students who cannot meet the prerequisite.

Richard West has worked closely with stakeholders from the Teacher Education Department as well as the IP&T Department to create a technology student assessment. The purpose of the assessment is to help students test their current level of technology ability and determine whether they have the technical skills to succeed in IPT286. Because this technology assessment will be required, students will enter IPT286 with a base level of technology skills, and all of the students will have a common starting point. There will still be students who are much more tech-savvy than others, but the huge divide between computer-literate and computer-illiterate students will be much smaller. Included in the assessment are many resource options where students can go for remediation, and the tone of the assessment is encouraging so that qualified teachers are not discouraged from applying to the program simply because they could not pass the assessment. Rather, the purpose of the assessment is to help students prepare so they can succeed once they are accepted into the program.

The plan is for the technology assessment to be implemented starting in the fall semester of 2004, so it will apply to students who are preparing their applications that semester to enter the program. While there are many options available for students who need to improve their technology skills (such as online tutorials, BYU classes, self-teaching with Microsoft Help Assistant, etc.), one option listed for the students is to take Office of Instructional Technology (OIT) Quickskills workshops. These are two-hour workshops, costing $10 each, that focus on a specific application or computer skill. The OIT has agreed to organize a series of seven workshops that would cover every unit of the elementary education technology requirement and that would cater specifically to incoming elementary education students. This workshop series will also be organized to begin in fall of 2004.

Once the technology prerequisite is in place, the structure of IPT286 will change. Instead of focusing equally on acquiring and integrating technology skills, the class will specialize in integration and on teaching more advanced technology skills. The students will be expected to already have basic skills, and if they do not, the burden will be on them to catch up and will not be on the teacher to specialize the instruction to accommodate them. For the majority of the students, IPT286 will be less of a cognitive overload because they will have already learned the computer skills and will only need to learn how to apply them. This will also free up the IPT286 instructors to teach more modeling sessions and offer more time in class for practicing integration, perhaps in lab or field settings.

Curriculum Change for Secondary Education Students

In coordination with the Teacher Education Department, a proposal has been submitted to the 31 Arts and Sciences Departments that participate in teacher education. This proposal requests an increase in the number of required IPT286 credit hours from one credit to two. Currently the amount of technology integration modeling that we are able to do with the students in one credit hour is very limited. If the proposal is approved, secondary students will be able to participate in a minimum of three modeling sessions rather than only one.

Introduction to Program Portfolios

The Teacher Education Department has recently determined that it will require students to create a program portfolio centered on the

INTASC standards. Currently the concepts related to developing a program portfolio are introduced in IPT286. Introducing the conceptual model for portfolios and the INTASC standards takes quite a bit of the course resources. It would be appropriate for the Teacher Education Department to assume the responsibility of introducing students to these conceptual frameworks in their program orientation. Then, in IPT286, we could build on this foundation by focusing on creating the shell of the portfolio and helping students add the first few artifacts and reflections. Recently this has been done successfully at the orientation for elementary education students. The department is also putting together a series of four workshops to follow up with students on portfolio skills such as selecting artifacts, writing good reflection documents, and managing electronic files.

CONCLUSIONS AND LESSONS LEARNED

As we look forward toward future redesigns of IPT286, we understand that the course will likely never be perfect, especially considering the rate at which technological possibilities change. However, we agree with Lockard and Abrams (2004) that computing technologies are "an essential part of the 'basics' of education in the twenty-first century." We hope to continue to work collaboratively with the Teacher Education Department to improve the course in order to help students think about how technology might be used to enhance their teaching. In conclusion we offer a few of our lessons we have learned in the redesign process.

1. Working collaboratively was essential to the process. The redesign process that we engaged in was enriched because of input from many different people. We received suggestions, ideas, and moral support from department and college stakeholders, students, past instructors, faculty colleagues, and many others. The outcome definitely would have been different had we relied on our knowledge and perspectives alone.
2. Professional development support was helpful. The PT3 grant provided support for attending conferences that had a huge influence in seeding innovative ideas from other institutions that found their way into the final course redesign. The grant also provided for brown-bag lunches which featured local ideas

about how technologies such as Inspiration or WebQuests were being integrated into the curriculum of faculty colleagues.

3. Institutional barriers are greater than expected. Making major curriculum changes is more challenging than the redesigners expected. Even simple curriculum changes may be virtually impossible on a reasonable timetable considering the number of departments that have to provide approval. Even something as seemingly simple as scheduling extra technology-equipped rooms was a major administrative process on campus that had to be done months in advance. Other administrative challenges included getting approval for course prerequisites and finding consensus on an approach to implementing program portfolios.

4. Iterative designs allowed us to move in the right direction. Using the concept of iterative design allowed us to make several incremental steps toward our ultimate goal without getting too bogged down and discouraged that progress was not being made. It has also facilitated the gathering of data from students and others that will help to make continual improvements.

REFERENCES

Graham, C. R., Webb, K., Hawkins, C. L., & Harlan, D. (2003). Linking mentoring and electronic teaching portfolios for Utah educators. *Journal of UASCD Theories & Practices in Supervision and Curriculum, 14,* 59-66.

Hargrave, C. P., & Hsu, Y.-S. (2000). Survey of instructional technology courses for preservice teachers. *Journal of Technology and Teacher Education, 8*(4), 303-314.

Lockard, J., & Abrams, P. (2004*). Computers for twenty-first century education* (6th ed.). Boston: Allyn & Bacon.

Merrill, P. F. (2003). Entering skills of students enrolling in an educational technology course. *Computers in the Schools, 20*(1/2), 105-111.

Mitchell, A. J., & Graham, C. R. (2003). Tool focus limits understanding of technology integration. Unpublished manuscript, Provo, UT.

Moursund, D., & Bielfeldt, T. (1999). *Will new teachers be prepared to teach in a digital age? A national survey on information technology in teacher education.* Santa Monica, CA: Milken Exchange on Education Technology.

National Center for Educational Statistics. (1999a). *Internet access in public schools and classrooms: 1994-1998.* Washington, DC: U.S. Department of Education.

National Center for Educational Statistics. (1999b). *Teacher quality: A report on the preparation and qualification of public school teachers.* Washington, DC: U.S. Department of Education.

National Center for Educational Statistics. (2003). *Internet access in U.S. Public schools and classrooms: 1994-2002.* Washington, DC: U.S. Department of Education.

Thornburg, D. D. (2003, December). *Technology in k-12 education: Envisioning a new future*. Paper presented at the Forum on Technology in Education: Envisioning the Future, Washington, DC.

Willis, J., & Mehlinger, H. (1996). Information technology and teacher education. In J. Sikula (Ed.), *Handbook of research on teacher education* (2nd ed., pp. 978-1029). New York: Macmillan.

Sharon Black

Designing and Teaming on the Outside: Extending PT3 Efforts Across Campus, Across Five Districts and Across the State

SUMMARY. Brigham Young University and its collaborative partners throughout Utah recognize that effectively "integrating technology" into pre-service programs and ultimately into K-12 classrooms requires *rethinking* both the potentials of technology and the programs themselves. And this rethinking needs to be done together. BYU (both School of Education and cross-campus faculty), five surrounding school districts, and the State Office of Education have a history of partnershipping, much but not all of which has been positive and productive. With receipt of a PT3 grant, these groups have undertaken a series of activities and projects to promote collaborative re-searching, rethinking and re-creating. This article traces some of the highlights of this experience and examines results. The author describes a memorable meeting that revealed closeness in goals and distance in understanding of these so-called partners, along with a pivotal series of workshops that revealed what can be accomplished when understanding is achieved. A 44-person trip to a technology conference in Las Vegas was a culminating activity for the renewed and rededicated partners; the author describes both personal and organizational aspects of this undertaking,

SHARON BLACK is Associate Professor, Department of Teacher Education, Brigham Young University, Provo, UT 84602 (E-mail: Sharon_black@byu.edu).

[Haworth co-indexing entry note]: "Designing and Teaming on the Outside: Extending PT3 Efforts Across Campus, Across Five Districts and Across the State." Black, Sharon. Co-published simultaneously in *Computers in the Schools* (The Haworth Press, Inc.) Vol. 21, No. 1/2, 2004, pp. 149-163; and: *Integrating Information Technology into the Teacher Education Curriculum: Process and Products of Change* (ed: Nancy Wentworth, Rodney Earle, and Michael L. Connell) The Haworth Press, Inc., 2004, pp. 149-163. Single or multiple copies of this article are available for a fee from The Haworth Document Delivery Service [1-800-HAWORTH, 9:00 a.m. - 5:00 p.m. (EST). E-mail address: docdelivery@haworthpress.com].

http://www.haworthpress.com/web/CITS
Digital Object Identifier: 10.1300/J025v21n01_11

along with its far-reaching results. A final section presents a series of benefits and accomplishments that have resulted from these collaborative rethinking activities. *[Article copies available for a fee from The Haworth Document Delivery Service: 1-800-HAWORTH. E-mail address: <docdelivery@ haworthpress.com> Website: <http://www.HaworthPress.com> © 2004 by The Haworth Press, Inc. All rights reserved.]*

KEYWORDS. Collaboration, partnership, mutual understanding and trust, technology integration, collaborative rethinking

In an address to the faculty and students of the David O. McKay School of Education, Dr. Charles Reigoluth urged faculty and students to go beyond "technology integration" to achieve "technology transformation," to use technology to "transform what goes on in the classroom." This transformation must be accomplished, he suggested, through interdisciplinary collaboration, through attempts by individuals representing diverse aspects of the educational enterprise to understand each other and enhance their interrelationships. As most of us know from painful experience, we cannot change one another's thinking from the outside by imposing requirements; Dr. Reigoluth taught us that we must work from the inside by *helping each other to rethink*. For many of us who have been involved in technology transformation at Brigham Young University and in nearby school districts, our progress has indeed been an experience in rethinking together.

We learned the language of collaborative rethinking 20 years ago when BYU formed a university-public school partnership with five school districts. We have learned actual processes of collaboration slowly (and sometimes painfully) over the years (Osguthorpe & Patterson, 1998). During the past three years we have found it necessary to reexamine our concepts and practices of collaboration and partnership as we have slowly come to recognize the many pieces and players involved in transforming conceptions and processes of technology integration at BYU and in the public schools which cooperate with us. This chapter will focus on groups and events that have been significant in the collaborative rethinking process.

ANTECEDENTS

Concepts of collaboration have long been integral to BYU's view of teacher education. Working with others is part of the University tradition, but efficiency and effectiveness have varied.

Partnerships

The BYU-Public School Partnership was formed in 1984, under the guidance and mentorship of John Goodlad (see Osguthorpe, Harris, Harris, & Black, 1995). The David O. McKay School of Education and the five public school districts agreed to be equal partners in joint efforts to simultaneously renew both teacher preparation and public school operation. Over the years a variety of seminars and conferences have been held, efforts have been made to achieve consistency in mentoring and supervising student teachers, the program of pre-service instruction/practica has been collaboratively revised, and numerous publications and presentations have been delivered. Genuine collaboration has been achieved in some places and in some ways, but gaps have been apparent, particularly concerning integration of technology.

In 1997, the partnership was extended to include arts and sciences departments across the university campus through the Center for the Improvement of Teacher Education and Schooling (CITES), a center of pedagogy modeled, like the original partnership, on the partnering ideals of Goodlad (see Goodlad, 1990). CITES became an administrative center for the partnership (Patterson, Michelli, & Pacheco, 1999), coordinating such projects as statewide instruction in balanced literacy; a distance education sequence in ESL leading to certification for in-service teachers; an expedited certification program in special education to meet a statewide shortage; special programs in conflict resolution and peaceable classrooms; and various science fairs and fine arts programs with broad participation. In some areas collaboration was progressing well.

Needs

But technology integration was an area in which collaboration was not progressing as it should. The university had a course introducing students to some basic computer skills that could be effectively used in classrooms. The districts had technology specialists who had skills, training, and ideas that could be effectively used in classrooms. Neither fully understood nor appreciated what the other had to offer, and neither was fully aware of the other's needs. Teachers in the arts and sciences departments participating in teacher preparation also had training, ideas, and experiences that would be valuable for teachers in classrooms, but they also were acting on their own–acknowledged minimally if at all by their supposed teacher preparation partners. There was a lot of frustration and very little collaboration. Certainly there was no group rethinking.

A Catalyst

Though not the only project to concern PT3 participants or to emerge from PT3 organization and funding, the need to develop electronic portfolios acted as a catalyst to get diverse participants involved. The Utah State Office of Education was moving toward a requirement (shortly to become official) that teachers would need to submit professional portfolios in order to obtain Level 2 licensure. Personnel from the State Office, technology specialists from the districts, and technology-oriented faculty and administrators from the School of Education all had their separate ideas of what portfolios should be and how they should be handled. Meetings were held, but the disparate ideas were not coming together very well. One district specialist moaned, "BYU's idea of cooperation is that they tell us what to do and we cooperate." The looming issue of the portfolio requirement gave all the groups a motivation to at least rethink their need to rethink.

THREE WHITEBOARDS

There is a very large table, with plenty of chairs, in the Dean's conference room at the School of Education, but no board space to write on. State Office personnel over technology, district technology specialists, and School of Education faculty with interests and responsibilities for technology were accustomed to meeting there and talking. But talking is not necessarily communicating, particularly if people are listening defensively, not carefully, to one another. During a rather typical meeting one afternoon, someone brought up the fact that none of the groups (all sitting somewhat isolated with their immediate colleagues) at the table really *knew* what the others were doing or wanted done concerning electronic portfolios–or any kind of portfolios for that matter. Someone suggested that written lists would be easier to coordinate than verbal expressions. The coordinator of the Teaching and Learning Support Center (BYU's computer lab) mentioned that the wireless classroom in the lab had three walls lined with whiteboards: One group could write on each wall.

So the combatants moved downstairs–literally and figuratively. State people, district people, and School of Education people were each assigned a wall, given a marker, and instructed to write in three columns: "What we are doing," "What we have to offer others," and "What we need from others." At the end of about 20 minutes, there was a lot of handwriting on the walls. Participants were startled at what they learned. University and district people had not realized how close and inevitable the portfolio requirement actually was, and they had not realized how much the State Office was actually doing to support portfolio development. State and district people had not realized what the University classes were actually teaching that could be easily adapted to support portfolios. The strengths of the district specialists had been unrecognized and underestimated by state and university people. It was surprising how often a "need" on one wall matched with a "contribution" on another. Group rethinking had begun.

COLLABORATIVE WORKSHOPS

From the group rethinking came the realization that more expert instruction was needed in working with electronic portfolios. With PT3 funding available to support such instruction, the group decided to ask Dr. Helen Barrett, recognized internationally for her work with electronic portfolios, to give a two-day series of workshops.

Participants

Invitations were issued to State Office personnel, district administrators and technology specialists, BYU administrators and faculty from the School of Education and from other campus departments supporting teacher preparation, technology/education personnel from other universities, and BYU students with special interests and expertise in technology. All groups came. There was standing room only.

One School of Education clinical faculty member was so suspicious and hostile toward adopting technology that she had told people emphatically, "I will NEVER use technology in MY classroom." When challenged to come and at least hear what Helen Barrett had to say, she slipped in to listen briefly so she would know what to argue against. By the end of the first session, she was excited to become involved with electronic portfolios. She is now one of the school's most enthusiastic technology advocates. Her ability to rethink became a strong example for many.

Large Group Rethinking

Dr. Barrett's workshop was a blend of presentations to the full group, meetings of small groups consisting of people with similar responsibilities and interests, and presentations by people who were using technology effectively, including district specialists. Complex change was a major theme for the overall group, with particular stress on aspects of rethinking such as common vision and collaborative decisions as follows:

- Developing a common vision
- Being willing to rethink and adapt individual visions
- Learning together
- Assessing skills and needs
- Assessing resources
- Developing a project design
- Providing adequate skill support
- Arranging adequate incentives and funding

Small Group Rethinking

With the large group primed to consider collaborative implementation of change, Dr. Barrett split the participants into small groups, somewhat homogeneous in the responsibilities and challenges with which they were involved: technology specialists, school of education methods faculty, school of education field faculty, various official "design teams," etc. The smaller groups were challenged to collaborate in examining (a) how to integrate electronic portfolios into the teacher education program, (b) what to teach and what to emphasize in the teaching, and (c) what assignments should be required of the students. Discussions were focused and purposeful, as group members knew they would be asked to give their results in writing. Notes from the various groups were later compiled, major themes extracted, and ideas compared. The collaboration worked so well that Dr. Barrett named this group collaboration procedure the "BYU Model." Some of the following themes emerged from these discussions:

- Need to introduce electronic portfolios early in the pre-service program
- Perspective that the portfolio is the context, technology is the tool; both exist to enhance content

- Perspective that the portfolio should be a natural extension of the students' work, not just another assignment
- Importance of incorporating INTASC standards
- Importance of reflection in compiling the portfolio
- Importance of having course assignments that require students to select and reflect
- Importance of all faculty modeling the use of technology
- Importance of feedback and assessment

Thus a large and varied group was on its way to collaborative rethinking of technology use as well as electronic portfolios.

A COLLABORATIVE TRIP

"Doing Vegas" together hardly seems on the surface like an important way to get state, district, and university people working together to rethink their integration of technology, but it turned out to be the strongest collaborative event of the PT3 experience. The conference for Connected Classroom was being held in Las Vegas, and grant administrators decided that a diverse group of technology participants would benefit from attending. Behind its occasionally casual façade, the trip was carefully planned, purposefully organized, and efficiently carried out. Figure 1 gives an overview of personnel and processes involved. Each will be discussed in turn.

Participants

A wide range of participants was invited, chosen for the groups and positions they represented as well as for their individual interest, expertise, and experience in using technology. The district technology specialists and additional public school personnel were not only not overlooked, they were solicited for particular skills and accomplishments. An assistant superintendent, a curriculum specialist, a mathematics coordinator, and several classroom teachers were included, along with those who had "technology" in their job titles. A group of fine arts instructors from campus–including visual arts, music, and dance–had been working for some time with public school teachers in one of the schools in the partnership to implement current methodology, including computers, in teaching the arts to elementary children. Several members of this group were included on the trip roster

FIGURE 1

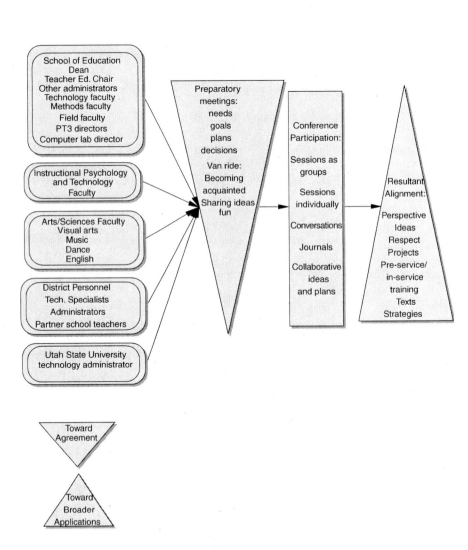

as well. The dean of the School of Education, an assistant dean, and other personnel from the dean's office were part of the group. Two department chairs–Teacher Education and Instructional Psychology and Technology–chose to go, along with professors from these departments, clinical faculty including district-university liaisons, and the director of the Teaching and Learning Support Center. The director of the Utah State University Resource Center also attended. (Rival college technologists get along much better than rival college football players.) With such a large and diverse entourage, chaos could have easily resulted; however, with thoughtful planning and careful execution, benefits were maximized and potential confusion prevented.

Planning and Anticipation

Although collaboration may seem to outsiders to be a natural process that should come together spontaneously, those who engage in it very much know that effective collaboration requires careful planning and structure. The organizers of the Las Vegas project engaged in a good deal of purposeful planning and coordination to be sure that maximum benefit in both collaboration and professional development would result.

Group organization and meetings. Recalling from the Barrett workshops the strength of getting people with complementing interests together, project organizers placed the participants in groups and asked them to meet prior to the trip to compare and assess needs and to make some decisions. School of Education administrators and faculty were assigned as a group, as were the arts teachers. For convenience in meeting and communicating, public school administrators, specialists, and teachers were organized according to district; the five districts in partnership with the university were all represented. Each group also included the district liaison who was responsible for university-district relationships and cooperation. Each group compiled a list of needs they had discerned and began thinking of ways these needs could be considered and met. Thus group members became acquainted with one another in terms of their roles and experiences concerning technology and technology integration, as well as getting a feel for one another's personalities and dispositions.

Journals. Recognizing the power of writing to crystallize thoughts and impressions, in addition to the importance of recording, project organizers furnished each participant with a planner-style looseleaf journal. Color-coded pages, inserted by the organizers, asked participants for comments in several designated areas:

Reflections on group collaborative experience

- Building trust
- Resolving differences
- Changes resulting from group ideas and interactions
- Ideas and insights developed by the group

Reflections on professional development

- Things you learned that you would apply in your classroom/administrative assignment
- Things you would share with your colleagues
- Things you think should be taught to cohort students

Respondents were told that the colored pages would be collected so that thinking could be studied and themes could be extracted and synthesized, but that the remainder of the journal—including the small binder and all of the pages that had originally been in it—were theirs as a gift.

Travel arrangements. Las Vegas is about a six-hour drive from Provo, Utah, the location of Brigham Young University. University vans seemed to be the most economical yet efficient way of transporting 44 people for that distance. Project organizers realized that some of the six hours should be spent in casual conversation, allowing people to get acquainted and establish personal bonds, but that some of the time could be effectively spent in professional conversation, allowing people to get to know one another's professional position, ideas, and experiences as well. Another decision was that participants would benefit from conversation with more than the eight or nine people who would be riding in a single van. So two rest stops were planned, at which time travelers would change vans to ride and interact with a new group of people. Specific in-van and inter-van activities were planned to facilitate the alternation of personal and professional conversation.

During the first part of the trip, participants were grouped into vans by their original collaborative group: teacher education professors, arts professors and teachers, various districts. All were given bags containing the conference programs, the journals, and a few items to make the trip comfortable. The groups were asked to begin by using their programs to plan as a group at least three sessions that they would attend together and discuss. The passengers considered the original lists from their meetings, and as groups they chose appropriate sessions and arranged times to meet and discuss what they were learning. To break up the seriousness of the conference planning, when the scheduling was completed everyone participated in an inter-van scavenger hunt, with prizes awarded to the inmates of the winning van at the first of the rest stops. Drawings were held for additional prizes.

The travelers were assigned to new van arrangements, with groups deliberately mixed in both professional assignment and geography. Again the groups participated first in an activity that involved professional communication, followed by an inter-van game that encouraged them to relax and enjoy each other on personal and social planes. At the final rest stop, participants returned to their original vans and simply conversed freely for the final period of the journey. Treats were passed around, and additional "door prizes" were drawn for among the vans. The group arrived in Las Vegas a little tired, but feeling like a unified group of colleagues and friends. Collaborative rethinking had already begun, and the climate was set for it to continue.

Conference Participation

It might seem odd that the discussion of planning and preliminaries is longer than the section on conference participation. This is really a natural proportion, as in well-conducted collaboration the preliminary steps often go on for weeks if not months in advance, and outcomes–if effective–may last indefinitely.

Pre-thinking. For many participants in this project, the preliminary aspects of collaborative rethinking and professional development began in hotel rooms and restaurants. Most were placed two to a room, and as all were in the same hotel and members of groups had become good friends, there were plenty of opportunities to talk–"off the record" as well as on. For example, sitting on adjoining beds with their conference schedules open, a science methods teacher and a writing instructor discussed merits, drawbacks, and possible applications of WebQuests prior to attending a session on WebQuests scheduled for the following morning. Their language arts compatriots a couple of floors above had also discussed WebQuests the night before, and all four were ready for focused listening and personal application as they attended the session together.

Experiencing. The sessions of the conference were informative and interesting, designed to be easy to apply in classrooms. Attendees learned about a wide variety of topics related to technology integration, ranging from questioning techniques for promoting critical and creative thinking to sites on the Internet to support grant writing. Sessions were as specific as WebQuests and as broad as assessment. Many related to

Internet research and Internet projects that could be easily integrated with classroom curricula. Some were more administrative in focus.

An additional experience in integrating technology was provided by a visit by many participants to a secondary mathematics classroom where successful technology integration was taking place. Assigned to a class of teenagers who had never been successful in mathematics classes in the past, the teacher had been determined to use technology-rich methods to reach these students. His school was not strong in computer resources; he had taken old computers from storerooms and put them to use. He used them for providing individual tutorials and practice, for dealing with questions, and for working with a Web site he had set up where students (and their parents) could access information about the class as well as mathematics assistance. One student told some of the group members that this was the first time she had ever been successful in math, that her experience in this class was totally different from anything she had been through in the past. Others seemed to be having similar experiences. Seeing the effectiveness of this teacher's use of technology (recycled technology and apparently recycled students) sparked rethinking for many of the observers.

Rethinking. The information, ideas, and applications received during the conference sessions were enhanced, enlarged, and expanded by frequent discussions among attendees. Lively conversation sprang up in the wake of a session on assessment, for example. During an evening pizza party, language arts teachers compared ideas related to teaching writing and research. The mock-market place at the Aladdin Hotel proved a satisfactory setting for some teachers to discuss their ideas and experiences, but the ear-splitting atmosphere at the Hard Rock Café was not conducive to anything very complex.

Journal writing had both of the effects the project organizers had desired. Putting experiences, impressions, feelings, and ideas into words caused the participants to examine their experiences more deliberately and thus to probe meaning behind their reactions. Themes were not difficult to extract and synthesize. Some of the most prevalent are given in Table 1.

CONTINUED TECHNOLOGY COLLABORATION

Teamwork and collaborative rethinking that began with lists of needs and contributions on whiteboards, continued through electronic portfolio workshops, and produced a 44-person conference excursion have continued through innumerable meetings and collaborative sessions

TABLE 1. Participants' Reflections on Collaboration and Development as Recorded in Journals

Collaboration	
Building trust	Personal relationships were built as colleagues shared experiences, feelings, and beliefs.
	Colleagues shared concerns and goals and looked for ways of meeting them.
	Colleagues learned to respect and value each other.
Resolving differences	Participants sensed differences, but did not feel a sense of conflict.
	Colleagues learned to see things from one another's perspective, to view things "through varying lenses."
	They found they actually had more commonalities than differences.
Professional Development	
Generating ideas for change	It is important to model innovative uses of technology: WebQuests, portfolio artifacts, innovative assessment.
	We must provide technical support to teachers and pre-service teachers–projects to bring them together, in-service instruction, computer support.
	Specific applications were mentioned: WebQuests, social studies core materials, math assessment, Web pages with parent help, electronic portfolios.
	Participants committed to work together.
Deciding what to pass on to others	Pre-service students need "real" experiences in using resources.
	Technology must be integrated in all content-area courses.
	Incentives, nurturing, and practice need to be provided.
	Everyone must be involved in helping children to think and use tools wisely.

through the three years of the PT3 grant. The events discussed in this chapter are a few of the more unusual and interesting highlights. Some of the instances of collaboration for technology that can be traced to these events are summarized:

1. People in the various districts are networking more effectively now than in many times past. They are listening to one another and sharing ideas. Many are trying out developments that have worked well in other districts.

2. Partnership districts are implementing additional technology training sessions for pre-service teachers and interns, in addition to in-service teachers in their districts.

3. Methods are being developed for collecting and using online data to enhance student instruction. Strategies for online testing are also being implemented and shared.

4. District technology specialists, representatives from the College of Fine Arts, and a number of professors who teach methods courses in the School of Education enrolled in the introductory technology course that is required of pre-service teachers, desiring to know what and how their students are being taught.

   a. There is now more consistency in expectations and assignments related to technology in the pre-service classes.

   b. There is more consistency between what pre-service students learn at the university and what they are able (and expected) to implement during their student teaching and other practicum experiences.

5. The fine arts group has created a series of technological tools and developments to enhance education in their field including the following:

   a. PowerPoint presentations: comprehensive art program, criticism model, review of art concepts in game format

   b. WebQuests on elementary and secondary levels

   c. Databases on effective teaching aid Web sites and art Web sites

6. Collaborative presentations have been given at a number of national conferences, and collaborative articles have been written involving university, Utah State Office of Education, and public school personnel.

7. The expectation that portfolios would become mandatory for Level 2 licensure in the State of Utah has become reality. The Utah State Office of Education, districts throughout the state, and universities throughout the state have undertaken to support pre-service and in-service teachers in preparing portfolios in electronic form, and there has been considerable cooperation and sharing of materials among them.

   a. An archive has been developed for storing materials in a working portfolio throughout pre-service programs so that final licensure portfolios can be easily completed.

b. Mentoring workshops are being held in which mentor teachers are coached in helping mentorees develop electronic portfolios and in using those portfolios as mentoring tools.

8. Personnel from several of the districts who had been involved in the Las Vegas trip chose to organize their participation at another national conference in a similar manner–with preplanning sessions, organized discussion en route, and purposeful conversations regarding sessions. They reported very positive results.

CONCLUSION

Rethinking can be a difficult undertaking, and collaborative rethinking can be more difficult still. With groups as diverse as teacher education professors and administrators, professors in the arts and sciences, public school teachers and technology specialists, and public school administrators (including the State Office of Education), rethinking technology integration can be daunting. But during the past three years extensive rethinking has taken place across these diverse but enthusiastic groups.

The external evaluator's report issued at the end of the third year of the PT3 grant concluded:

> An exceptionally strong component of this grant was the close collaboration among the university, the public schools, the Utah State Department of Education, and other educational partners. BYU has done a wonderful job in reaching out to the broader educational community, and much of the lasting effects of the grant will be due to this effort.

Representatives of this broader educational community affirm that they have benefited and continue to benefit from the activities and collaborative rethinking undertaken under this grant. Plans are in place for such collaboration to continue.

REFERENCES

Goodlad, J. I. (1990). *Teachers for our nation's schools.* San Francisco: Jossey-Bass.

Osguthorpe, R. T., Harris, R. C., Harris, M. F., & Black, S. (1995). *Partner schools: Centers for educational renewal.* San Francisco: Jossey-Bass.

Osguthorpe, R. T., & Patterson, R. S. (1998). *Balancing the tensions of change: Eight keys to collaborative educational renewal.* Thousand Oaks, CA: Corwin Press.

Patterson, R. S., Michelli, N. M., & Pacheco, A. (1999). *Centers of pedagogy: New structures for educational renewal.* San Francisco: Jossey-Bass.

Michael L. Connell
D. LaMont Johnson

The View from Outside: 2000-2003

SUMMARY. In 1999, the Federal Department of Education began the PT3 initiative. The goal of that initiative was to transform teacher education programs across the country to ensure that new teachers would enter the classroom prepared to effectively integrate information technology. The BYU McKay School of Education demonstrated that university faculty, when provided with strong leadership and appropriate opportunities, will embrace and implement new ideas. *[Article copies available for a fee from The Haworth Document Delivery Service: 1-800-HAWORTH. E-mail address: <docdelivery@haworthpress.com> Website: <http://www.HaworthPress.com> © 2004 by The Haworth Press, Inc. All rights reserved.]*

KEYWORDS. Professional development, instructional technology, technology integration, leadership teams

As external evaluators for Brigham Young University's PT3 grant we were granted a unique view into what was, in many ways, a unique and powerful reformation of teacher education using technology as a

MICHAEL L. CONNELL is Associate Professor, Department of Curriculum and Instruction, University of Houston, Houston, TX 77069-5872 (E-mail: Mkahnl@aol.com).
D. LAMONT JOHNSON is Editor of *Computers in the Schools* and Professor, Counseling & Educational Psychology Department, University of Nevada, Reno, Reno, NV 89557 (E-mail: ljohnson@unr.edu).

[Haworth co-indexing entry note]: "The View from Outside: 2000-2003." Connell, Michael L., and D. LaMont Johnson. Co-published simultaneously in *Computers in the Schools* (The Haworth Press, Inc.) Vol. 21, No. 1/2, 2004, pp. 165-183; and: *Integrating Information Technology into the Teacher Education Curriculum: Process and Products of Change* (ed: Nancy Wentworth, Rodney Earle, and Michael L. Connell) The Haworth Press, Inc., 2004, pp. 165-183. Single or multiple copies of this article are available for a fee from The Haworth Document Delivery Service [1-800-HAWORTH, 9:00 a.m. - 5:00 p.m. (EST). E-mail address: docdelivery@haworthpress.com].

http://www.haworthpress.com/web/CITS
© 2004 by The Haworth Press, Inc. All rights reserved.
Digital Object Identifier: 10.1300/J025v21n01_12

driving force. As evaluators we were highly impressed with what BYU accomplished. It is our intent in this article to highlight and expand on the more salient of these accomplishments. Although the PT3 grant is now over, its impact will linger on. It is our hope that the information in this article will provide specific suggestions for the continuing role of instructional technology as a change agent within teacher education so that the entire field might benefit from the successes achieved by Brigham Young University.

EVALUATION FOCUS

In preparing this article we were guided by the evaluative goals identi-fied in cooperation with the principal investigators of the grant during the summer of 1999–prior to the initiation of the external evaluation. The evaluative goals targeted specifically for the external evaluators were based on Stufflebeam's (1971) CIPP evaluation model. Our evaluation goals were also grounded in the principles of knowledge-based evaluation pro-posed by Connell (2002). In order to evaluate the BYU PT3 project, we in-vestigated the influence of the grant in two areas: changes in student use of technology in their educational endeavors and changes in faculty percep-tions regarding the use of technology in teaching and learning.

The first investigative area, changes in student use of technology in their educational endeavors, resulted in the creation of the following questions that served as guideposts for conducting much of the external evaluation:

1. How are BYU faculty members integrating technology into their existing course syllabi?
2. How often do BYU faculty members require students to work on a technology project as part of regular course work?
3. To what degree do BYU faculty members require students to produce technology-enhanced lessons covering public school content?

The second investigative area, changes in faculty perceptions regard-ing the use of technology in teaching and learning, led to the creation of a fourth evaluation question:

4. To what extent did faculty members' perceptions change with regard to technology and the degree to which BYU students should incorporate technology into their learning experiences?

Format of Structured Interview

During the three-year evaluation period reported in this article we conducted a parallel series of discussions with faculty and support staff using a set of structured interview questions. These questions proved to provide crucial insights into both student uses of technology and faculty perceptions. These questions proved to be extremely valuable as "conversation starters," facilitating discussion with both individual faculty and design team members. We were able during this three-year process to preserve the data integrity of each year and to expand on this database over time as new elements were observed.

The questions used in the structured interview follow:

- What was your previous instructional technology (IT) background?
- What were your thoughts concerning IT prior to the grant?
- What grant-related activities influenced your thinking, and how?
- What non-grant-related activities influenced your thinking?
- Which activities had the greater impact on your thinking, grant related or non-grant related?
- How would you categorize your feelings around IT at this point?
- What can you honestly picture yourself doing with IT in five years?
- How have your students incorporated IT in their field experiences? (if applicable)
- How often do your students use IT in their classroom experiences at this point?
- Describe their activities, if appropriate.
- How often did your students use IT in their classroom experiences prior to the grant?
- To what extent did the grant affect this?
- Anything else you would like us to know, or wish we did not know?

While we used these questions as the basis for a structured interview, we occasionally varied from these questions during informal discussions. In actual practice, the structured interview questions came to serve as a common starting point for such discussions. Once this core area of interest was addressed, the discussions became more wide ranging and dealt with related topics of specific interest to the faculty members. These expanded discussions provided valuable insights into progress toward grant goals, and served to influence and direct our evaluation.

FINDINGS FROM INTERVIEWS

Technology Skills Held by Faculty

Evaluation results for the first two years of the grant showed that many of the faculty had entered into the grant with at least some minimal technology background. As might be expected, word processing led the list of skills, with 84% of the reporting faculty indicating a high level of proficiency. The next most commonly reported skills in this same time period were the use of PowerPoint to create presentations, e-mail uses, and simple Internet searches. These skills were mentioned so often that they were jokingly referred to as the "Big Four" by several of the participants in our earlier interviews.

We noted at that time that, although these were commendable skills, they might indicate a reliance on knowledge presentations over knowledge construction as a primary teaching method. It was most heartening to see how this picture changed during the last grant year. The "Big Four" reported in the second-year report—word-processing, PowerPoint, e-mail, and Internet searches—seemed to be accepted as being so basic and ubiquitous by the final year that they did not even deserve mention by faculty. On the few occasions when we prompted for them, we were rewarded with comments similar to "Well of course we can do that."

By the end of the grant, the skills mentioned in the faculty interviews revealed several interesting patterns, falling more along the lines of knowledge and information generation than along the lines of presentation of canned resources. We believe that a significant shift in both personal use and practicing pedagogy occurred during the final project year. This shift is clearly evident in Figure 1, where it can be seen that 44% of the faculty specifically mentioned electronic portfolios during the third-year interviews. The practice of creating electronic portfolios requires a diverse and well-developed set of skills that were not nearly as prevalent in preceding years. A similar case may be presented for the 31% of the faculty who mentioned the use of WebQuests in their own instruction. Of the "Big Four" PowerPoint still remained a major player, with 25% of the faculty specifically mentioning it. Even PowerPoint was mentioned in a different context, however, with faculty describing insertion of video clips and the use of PowerPoint as an organizing–not presenting–medium.

Figure 1 was created from self-reports of the 25 faculty (describing 51 skills) from the second-year evaluation and 16 faculty (describing 36 skills) in the final set of interviews. From this perspective it is possible to observe the marked and significant changes in skill focus over the final two years of the grant.

A rather surprising finding from the second-year interviews was that many faculty shared with us the perception that technology was best suited to a single skill or task, rather than reflecting the rich and near plastic possibilities to which information technology might be applied. At that time there was a large number of faculty who, in their own minds, possessed a single skill related to instructional technology. This situation changed significantly during the final year. As Figure 2 illustrates, the vast majority of those responding indicated that they rou-

FIGURE 1. Self-report of IT skill types for year two and year three.

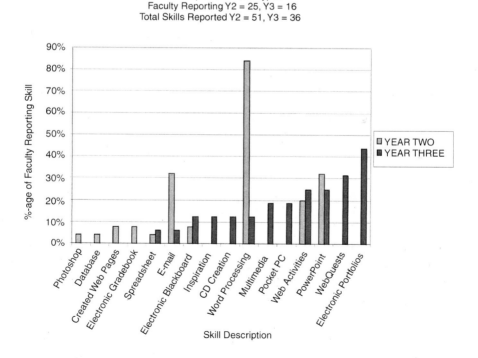

Self-Report of IT Skill Types
Faculty Reporting Y2 = 25, Y3 = 16
Total Skills Reported Y2 = 51, Y3 = 36

tinely used at least four disparate skill sets in their instruction. The results shown in Figure 2 suggest that the use of computers progressed a long way from being viewed as word-processing and e-mail devices. IT came to be broadly integrated into many more aspects of instructional planning and preparation. Far from being viewed as a single tool, the computer was increasingly viewed as a multifaceted tool with a variety of applications and associated skill sets.

Perspectives on Information Technology

It was markedly clear to each evaluator, based on responses received during each of three yearly evaluations, that the faculty in the McKay School of Education at BYU made tremendous progress in their perspectives on how information technology can be used to enhance teaching and learning. Changes in this perspective are illustrated by contrasting some of the interview responses of the third-year evaluation with the comments made by one faculty member during the first-year

FIGURE 2. Self-report of number of skills held by faculty.

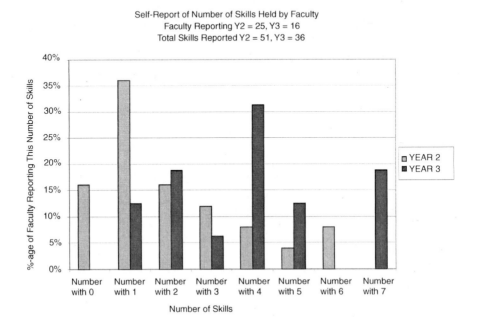

Self-Report of Number of Skills Held by Faculty
Faculty Reporting Y2 = 25, Y3 = 16
Total Skills Reported Y2 = 51, Y3 = 36

interviews. This faculty member, when asked about his perspectives on information technology, honestly stated, "I simply didn't think about it."

By the second year of the grant, the level of awareness and discourse regarding the use of technology in teaching and learning were much higher. It would be fair, however, to classify most of the faculty's perceptions on technology as being predominately rule-driven, or task-driven. At this time, the faculty tended to view technology as a technological tool, and if they viewed it as a useful aid to help them in performing a needed task, they would be willing to give it a try. With the exception of the early adopters, technology usage and integration into classes and student expectations appears to have been driven by awareness of tools paralleling the individual faculty member's preferred teaching methodology.

By the third year of the grant there was growing evidence that many faculty had progressed into what Maddux, Johnson, and Willis (2001) have described as Type II uses of technology. These authors have described a dichotomy of technology uses in education where the two extremes are labeled Type I and Type II. Type I applications of technology involve ways to make tasks easier, quicker, or otherwise more efficient while continuing to teach in traditional ways. Type II applications, on the other hand, tend to promote new and better methods of teaching and learning, methods that would not be available without technology. Type II uses of technology are typified by ways of using technology that tend to transform the instructional paradigm, restructure the organization of the classroom, and allow educators to make use of technology to do things differently.

The majority of School of Education faculty had entered the grant knowing word-processing and e-mail skills and indicated that it was the Internet and its tremendous information gathering potential that was their greatest motivation for expanded inclusion of technology. By year three, most faculty were looking far beyond such relatively simplistic tasks as surfing the Internet for information and were actively using WebQuests as a teaching and learning tool. Much of this increased sophistication seems to be centered on one of the grant outcomes, which was an initiative relating to electronic portfolios and their importance within the state licensing process for teachers within the state of Utah. Regardless of what format is finally adopted for this initiative, it is clear that as the BYU professors worked to enable their students to meet this extremely important goal, their own level of technical sophistication was enhanced.

The impact the grant had on faculty perceptions and use of technology would be hard to underestimate. One faculty member said:

> The grant has changed the use of instructional technology in the BYU School of Education. It is obvious that there is more emphasis here in the School of Education than anywhere on campus. When I go to other general university classes, the education students stand out when it comes to making presentations and using instructional technology.

Our evaluation results indicate that BYU faculty perceptions of instructional technology progressed from being viewed as complex and too time consuming, to being viewed as easy and efficient. In the words of one faculty member: "I see instructional technology as more simplified now. For me it went from being an external thing to a tool that can enhance teaching and learning." The central role of instructional technology was reflected in many of the interviews where it was described as "a resource to supplement and improve what we do" and "I have learned to make the link between instructional technology and the students."

It is fair to say that the vast majority of faculty we spoke with were extremely positive regarding both technology and their role within the grant. Comments such as "Instructional technology has changed the whole way I teach, write, and prepare for classes–now it is just part of what I do" and "I have seen the level of teaching with instructional technology and could never think about teaching without it" were typical.

It is important to note that this belief was not merely held by the early adopters or the more junior faculty. Several of the senior faculty indicated that the technology support they had received had invigorated their teaching. One senior faculty member said:

> The PT3 grant gave me opportunities to develop some of the things I am now using. What I am doing in my courses has changed phenomenally. It has also changed how I look at professional development.

Grant Activities Influencing Thinking

The grant leadership is to be commended for the manner in which the grant was administered, and it is clear that the vision and guidance of this leadership team contributed much to the success of the grant. The national leadership of the PT3 grant effort emphasized from the beginning that they wanted to offer flexibility to grant recipients. BYU was one grant recipient that truly took advantage of this flexibility and made it work. Some of the most dramatic successes of the grant were almost serendipitous and would not have happened in a very tightly controlled situation.

To gain a perspective regarding some of the grant activities most appreciated by faculty see Figure 3, which tabulates some of the grant-related items specifically mentioned by the faculty that influenced their thinking.

Far and away the single event that was viewed as having the greatest impact was the conference support offered to faculty. Furthermore, this support for conference attendance provided several additional payoffs for BYU. During the course of the grant the strong presence of faculty from BYU at the international conferences of the Society for Information Technology & Teacher Education (SITE) advanced the reputation

FIGURE 3. Grant activities mentioned as influencing use and perception of technology.

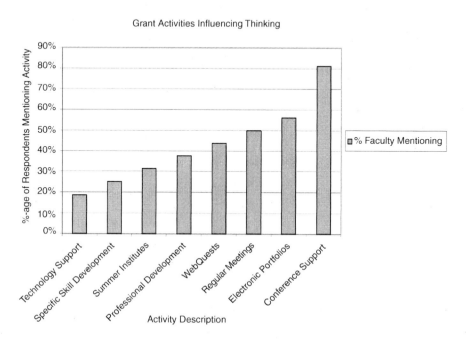

of BYU as a leader in the field of information technology in teacher education. This support, when coupled with the regular meetings sponsored by the grant, also served to build a strong community of faculty who now view one another in a markedly different fashion. One faculty member stated:

> In my opinion, the greatest benefit of the PT3 grant has been the sense of community that has been created through it. This has been very important. It has brought people from different programs together and got them talking, which was not happening before. For example, I have been very involved in the teacher education program. In many cases, we no longer see each other as interfering in each other's domain.

In keeping with the increased focus on technology within the state of Utah, it is not surprising that many faculty expressed feelings such as "One of the great influences of the grant has come about in the way it has involved the public schools." This impact clearly demonstrates the influence BYU has had in the larger community. This was clearly stated by a state office employee:

> The Y's PT3 grant enabled some of the things we are doing at the state department. It helped us formalize our instrument for entry-level teachers. Each district will receive portfolios for the first year of teaching. So, the training and sustained effort of BYU through the PT3 grant became a catalyst for this effort all across the state. PT3 was instrumental in making electronic portfolios a statewide effort instead of just an institutional (BYU) effort, which it could have become if BYU had not reached out.

If the old saying "it takes a very good meeting to be better than no meeting at all" has merit, it should be noted that in the eyes of 50% of the faculty interviewed, the BYU PT3 grant-related meetings were indeed very good. BYU held planning meetings, summer institutes, and a wide series of brown bag technology meetings. Together, these meetings provided for an ongoing dialogue concerning technology to be held and built a strong sense of community among the technology-using faculty.

The summer institutes served a pivotal role in focusing faculty attention on specific techniques and tools and were foundational to the grant's success. Figure 1 shows that the two skill types mentioned most often by faculty involved WebQuests and electronic portfolios–both topics of summer institutes. These institutes were mentioned often in comments such as "The WebQuest workshop during summer 2002 was very helpful and the brown bag sessions during the year have been very helpful as well" and "The summer workshop on using WebQuests had a very strong influence on our teaching and on our thinking about instructional technology."

Despite the increased sophistication of the faculty, the need for basic technology support and specific skill development remained a priority for faculty and enabled many of the activities first encountered within the summer workshops. Two faculty members said:

> We now have our students create digital portfolios. We used to do this with paper, but because of Helen Barrett's workshop during the first year of the PT3 grant, we have developed a system for them to do electronic portfolios.

Overall the perceived levels of technical support seemed adequate for the attainment of the goals of the grant. One faculty member put it this way: "I think we are going to be able to do some good things here at BYU. We have some good technology and some good support." The ongoing skills development was also mentioned as an appreciated item: "I appreciated the workshops and training opportunities. There has been some opportunity to learn nearly every month during the grant."

Non-Grant Activities Influencing Thinking

Faculty members who participated in the BYU PT3 grant had opportunities to participate in a variety of activities that were not directly sponsored by the grant. We refer to these activities as non-grant activities and we have summarized their influence on faculty members in Figure 4. One of the more interesting of these non-grant activities was the Pocket PC project. This activity consisted of training faculty members to use pocket computers and helping them understand potential educational uses of pocket computers.

The pocket computer clearly seems to be an enabling tool, which is currently leveraging forward the skills and inclinations which the PT3 grant created within the faculty. The university is also to be commended for the significant support offered at both the department and university levels. This support, together with the site licensing of the software pro-

FIGURE 4. Non-grant activities most influencing faculty.

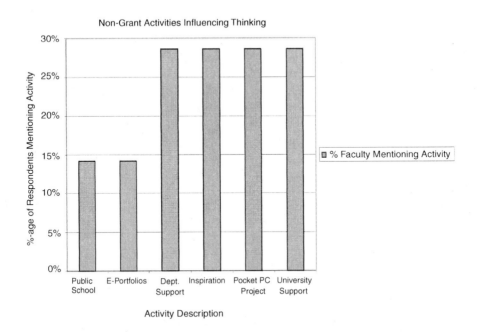

gram *Inspiration* and its subsequent availability to faculty, were highly valued by faculty.

The faculty seemed to be clearly aware of the new requirement for electronic portfolios and the impact that this has had within the state. They cited the increased expectations on the part of the public schools and the state office regarding portfolios, in particular, as being an important driving force in their change process.

Student Uses of Technology in Field-Based Settings

Student use of technology in the field expanded to include a broad array of skills and knowledge. Many of these are directly related to the creation and maintenance of electronic portfolios, others are more pedagogical in nature and reflect emerging experience in instructional planning and implementation. Figure 5 summarizes those skills explicitly mentioned as being required by those we interviewed.

FIGURE 5. Student uses of technology in field-based settings.

Student Uses of Technology in Field-Based Settings

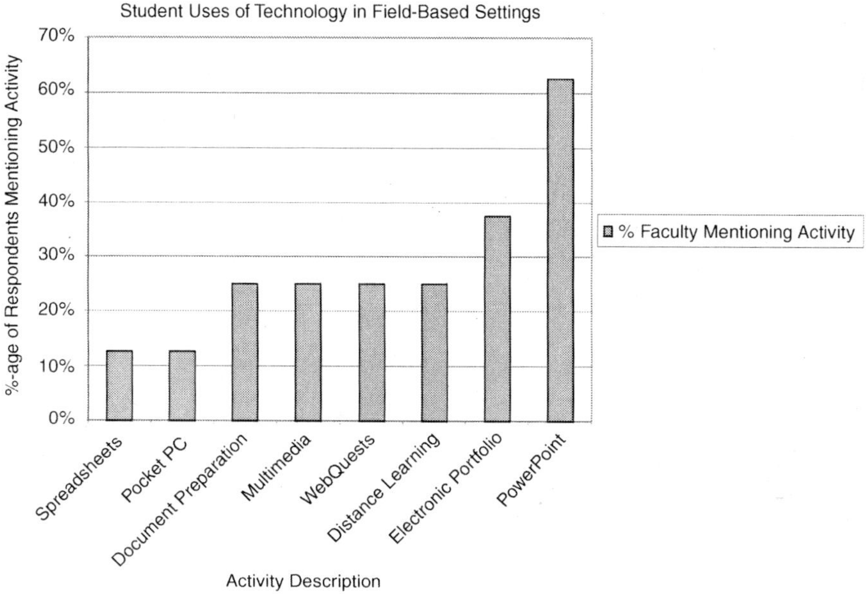

It is clear that electronic portfolios weighed heavily on the minds of teacher candidates. It is also not surprising that many of the skills expressed as being used in the field reflect this focus. This was expressed very clearly by faculty, one of whom put it this way:

> We have total synchronization of what they are learning in their courses and what they are doing out in the districts. We have coordinated our electronic portfolios with what the state department is doing state-wide. One of the great benefits of having the students do electronic portfolios has been the skills they have learned that can carry over to other areas of their teaching and learning.

Student Uses of Technology in Classroom Settings

As might be expected, the majority of skills required of students by faculty for in-class performance were similar to those expected for field-based performance. Figure 6 shows the major uses identified as being required by faculty.

FIGURE 6. Student uses of technology in classroom settings.

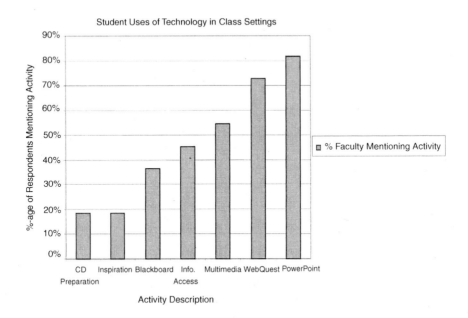

The progress of student expectations expressed by faculty clearly emerged over the three years of the grant. Initially there was the expectation that students would be able to word process; this was followed by the use of the Web. By the final year of the project we began to hear comments such as:

> We used to do a paper on infusing technology into our courses. Our students now expect it. We find that our students are much more prepared to use technology and expect to use technology as part of our courses.

The PT3 grant has clearly changed instruction, as evidenced by the following comment:

> It used to be mostly a lecture course taught in a large lecture hall with a separate lab experience. I have been able to move it more toward a modeling of integration into the curriculum. The course has been closely aligned with the PT3 grant and the design teams. And

we have initiated a module where the students design and build an electronic portfolio.

Conference Attendance and Grant Goals

Given the large number of faculty who expressed their appreciation for grant support, a closer look was taken regarding the influence on the overall success of the grant of faculty members being supported in their attendance at SITE conferences. An electronic search for references to, and papers authored and presented by, BYU faculty was made using the SITE proceedings for 2001, 2002 and 2003 as a data source (see Figure 7).

There were several important features noted: First, the number of faculty from BYU represented at the SITE conferences doubled between the first and third years of the grant. The opportunity to attend and interact with other scholars and teacher educators from around the world was mentioned by many of the faculty as a major strength of their grant involvement.

Furthermore, the number of papers published in the proceedings (as opposed to those papers that were merely presented without being published) likewise underwent a near tripling during this same time frame. Given the crucial role of academic publishing in the lives of most professors, and the concurrent rise in reputation for the institutions which they represent, this increased level of perceived scholarly activity is an extremely important aspect of the PT3 grant's performance.

Present Feelings Regarding Technology in Education

It becomes quickly obvious when interviewing faculty members who participated in the BYU PT3 grant that, over the three-year period, faculty members developed strong, positive feelings for the role of technology in teaching and learning. Much of this positive feeling has been developed through the willingness of the faculty to work hard at developing their knowledge and skills and through their willingness to step out and try new things. A sampling of these positive feelings as expressed by faculty members follows:

- "We are to the point where we are always thinking about how we can better use and model technology."
- "I have learned to make the link between IT and the students."
- "Dave's participation in the PT3 grant has provided his students with the opportunity to learn about IT and to use it in their learning and in their teaching."

- "I feel very positive, we just need to keep it going."
- "The students have learned a lot about evaluation by going through the self-reflection part of the electronic portfolio experience."
- "The PT3 grant has had a broad influence. It has influenced the BYU College of Education, the university, the public schools, and the state."
- "I have nothing more to offer other than to say I think the grant has been a great success and that it has really helped me to appreciate the power of IT and has helped me to develop some skills so that I can use it more effectively."
- "I now see IT as a resource to supplement and improve what we do."

CONCLUSION

The wide-ranging effect of this grant was phenomenal. We can, without hesitation, say that it has had an impact on teaching and learning in

FIGURE 7. BYU's representation at the annual SITE conference.

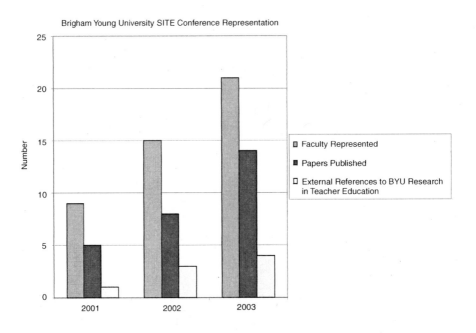

all departments and programs in the McKay School of Education, across other colleges within the university, in several surrounding school districts, and across the state of Utah. It would be hard to find another PT3 implementation grant that has had such a profound impact on pre-service teacher education.

In 1999, the U.S. Department of Education began the PT3 initiative. The goal of that initiative was to transform teacher education programs across the country to ensure that new teachers would enter the classroom prepared to effectively integrate information technology. Educators across America realized that change of this magnitude presented a formidable challenge. Much of the challenge came from long experience in bringing about change in institutions of higher learning where faculty tend to be fiercely independent and notoriously resistant to outside pressure. The BYU McKay School of Education, however, demonstrated that university faculty, when provided with strong leadership and appropriate opportunities, will embrace and implement new ideas.

The degree to which faculty bought into the BYU grant was exceptional. When you find people from every department within the McKay School of Education and others across campus participating and feeling that they were enriched by various grant-related experiences, you know this grant did some special things.

After carefully observing the BYU PT3 grant for three years, we concluded that one of its greatest strengths was the flexibility practiced by the leadership teams. The national leadership of the PT3 initiative emphasized from the beginning that they wanted to offer flexibility to grant recipients. BYU was one grant recipient that truly took advantage of this opportunity and made it work. Some of the most dramatic successes of the grant were serendipitous and would not have happened in a more tightly structured situation.

The strengths and abilities demonstrated by the leadership team in using grant monies to enable unforeseen enrichment opportunities are worthy of special commendation. As was noted earlier, by being sensitive to the emerging needs of faculty and various opportunities, they accomplished more serendipitously with grant funds than many universities have through careful advanced planning.

Another great strength of the BYU PT3 grant was the continued optimism of the grant leadership team and indeed of the participating faculty and staff. In the second year, several problems arose relating to a perceived diminishing of focus on the design team aspect of the grant, which was a key element in the grant proposal, and a growing gap between the clinical faculty and the tenured faculty associated with the grant. Rather than arguing these points, the grant leadership team addressed them during the third and final year of the grant and the problems essentially disappeared. The overall tenor of the BYU PT3 grant was always positive. Members of the leadership team and most of the faculty and staff associated with the grant never seemed to get discouraged. They embraced new challenges and new opportunities with equal fervor.

An exceptionally strong component of this grant was the close collaboration among the university, the public schools, the Utah State Department of Education, and other educational partners. BYU did a wonderful job in reaching out to the broader educational community and much of the lasting effects of the grant will be because of this effort.

As we look back on the three years of this BYU PT3 grant we can, without hesitation, state that it did an exceptional job in meeting the goals established in the PT3 effort. New teachers leaving BYU were much better prepared to integrate information technology into their new classrooms, and school districts across the state of Utah will be much better prepared to offer these new teachers opportunities to do so.

A listing of some of the major accomplishments of the BYU PT3 grant follows:

- Faculty members moved from a technology proficiency level that emphasized the acquisition of basic skills such as word processing to a point where basic skills were ubiquitous and viewed as rudimentary requirements for functioning as an educator.
- The emphasis on educational technology applications moved from a point where they were seen as supplementary to a point where they were seen as integral to the basic functions of planning and delivering instruction.
- Many faculty members moved from a state where they did not consider technology as part of the teaching and learning process to a point where they think of certain technology tools in the same way they used to think of pencils, paper, and chalk boards—essential basic tools.
- Using the Maddux, Johnson, and Willis (2001) Type I and Type II dichotomy of uses of technology, many BYU faculty members have moved from Type I uses to Type II uses.
- Many faculty and support personnel were exposed to national and international trends and issues relating to information technology in education by attending international conferences.

- The level of faculty publication and conference presentation, and hence increased exposure for BYU's programs and accomplishments, was greatly increased through publishing and conference presentation opportunities facilitated by the PT3 grant.
- Faculty members greatly increased their expectations for student use of technology.
- Pre-service teachers left the teacher education program better prepared in terms of skills and knowledge to integrate information technology into their classrooms.

REFERENCES

Connell, M. L. (2002). Knowledge-based evaluation. *Journal of Technology and Teacher Education. 10*(1), 17-26.

Maddux, C. D., Johnson, D. L., & Willis, J. W. (2001). *Educational computing: Learning with tomorrow's technologies* (3rd ed.). Boston: Allyn & Bacon.

Stufflebeam, D. L. (1971). *Educational evaluation and decision making*. Itaska, IL: Peacock Publishing.

Index

Accountability, 52
Action research, 43-57
  as approach, 45-46
  climate for, 51
  conclusions, 56-57
  definition, 46-47
  image of teacher, 48-49
  learning process reassessment,
    49-50
  lessons learned, 53-56
  process, 47-51
  results, 51-52
  teamwork, 50
Administrative policies, toward
    electronic portfolios, 110
Apple Computer, 8
Athletics and co-curricular
    experiences, 52
Attitudes, toward electronic portfolios,
    99

Balanced Literacy Instruction, 34-35
Barrett, Dr. Helen, 100-101,153-155
BlackBoard, 120
Brigham Young University McKay
    School of Education, 3-7
Bronowski, Jacob, 44
BYU PT3 implementation grant. *See*
    PT3 program

Casio, 8
Center for the Improvement of Teacher
    Education and Schooling
    (CITES), 151
Change

attitudes toward, 44-45,74
mature teacher/educators and,
    73-84
Character education/citizenship, 52
CITES, 151
Co-curricular experiences, 52
Collaboration
  among design teams, 22
  conclusions, 163
  conference participation, 159-160
  Connected Classroom Conference
    (Las Vegas), 155-160
  continuation of, 160-163
  facilities and, 152-153
  group rethinking, 153-155
  planning and anticipation for,
    157-159
  with public schools, 7,149-163
  workshops, 153-155
Connected Classroom Conference (Las
    Vegas), 9-10,30,155-160
Context and belief, 27
Course design, 127-148
  background and context, 129-130
  conclusions and lessons learned,
    146-147
  curriculum change for secondary
    education students, 145
  first redesign limitations, 142-143
  first redesign strengths, 140-142
  introduction to program portfolios,
    145-146
  IPT286 first redesign, 137-143
  IPT286 original design, 133-137
  IPT286 second redesign, 143-146
  modeling sessions, 140
  original design limitations, 136-137

original design strengths, 136
process overview, 130-133
technology skills prerequisites,
143-145
Course portfolios, 109
Curriculum design teams, 1-14,15-23.
See also Faculty design teams
Curriculum development, 9-11,52

Democracy and Education (Dewey),
29-30

Early Years Enhancement, 97,103-104
Electronic portfolios
Alaskan example, 100-101
breakdowns and near breakdowns,
98-99
breaks, 97-98
breaks passed forward, 104-109
breakthroughs, 99-104
conclusions, 112-113
course, 109
course design and, 145-146
cross-state, 95-113
Early Years Enhancement, 97,
103-104
East Coast examples, 100
evolution, 85-95
èxit, 109
faculty attitudes, 99
faculty experiences, 110-111
INTASC standards and, 106,108
layered system, 105-107
lessons learned, 109-112
NCATE and, 98
Nebo School District example,
101-103
presentation, 107,109
program, 109
student experiences, 111-112
Utah Education Network, 97-98
working, 107-109

Evaluation, 52
external, 165-183. *See also* External
evaluation
situated, 7-8
Evendon, Nancy, 101-103
Èxit portfolios, 109
External evaluation, 165-183
conclusions, 180-183
conference attendance and grant
goals, 179
faculty technology skills, 168-170
focus of, 166-168
grant activities influencing
thinking, 172-175
interview format, 167-168
non-grant activities influencing
thinking, 175-176
perspectives on information
technology, 170-172
present feelings, 179-180
student technology use: classroom
settings, 177-179
student technology use: field-based
settings, 176-177

Faculty, electronic portfolio
experiences, 110-111
Faculty-as-Students Model, 135. *See
also* Professional
development
Faculty design teams, 8-12
collaboration among, 22
conclusion, 12-13,22-23
curriculum development, 9-11
definition, 17-18
development of, 8-9
faculty-led initiative, 19-20
flexible support structures, 20-21
naturally occurring analyses, 20
needs analysis, 18-19
personal commitment, 21-22
for problem-based learning, 28-38
sustainability, 11-12
Faculty expertise, 5

Handheld computers, 65,68,175-176
HTML coding, 121,123,124
HyperStudio, 121,123

Instructional technology course, 10-11
Instructional units, 6-7
INTASC standards, 106,108,146
INTEL Teach the Future, 8
Interstate New Teachers Assessment
    and Support Consortium. *See*
    INTASC
ISTE standards, 8

Learning curve, for mature educators,
    73-84
Learning process, 48-49
Levels of Technology Integration
    (Moersch), 12

Mature educators
    benefits and barriers to, 80-83
    learning curve, 73-84
    mathematics, 77-79
    science, 75-77
    university and PT3 support, 79-80
Mentoring, 7
Moersch's Levels of Technology
    Integration, 12
Moral Dimensions of Teaching
    (Goodlad), 52
Multimedia presentations, 6. *See also*
    Electronic portfolios
National Board for Professional
    Teaching Standards
    (NBPTS), 112
NCATE standards, 4-7
Nebo School District, 101-103

On the Path (video), 47

Partnerships, 149-163

antecedents, 150-152
    with public schools. *See also*
        Collaboration
Personal commitment, 21-22
Planning, 52
Portfolios
    course, 109
    electronic. *See* Electronic portfolios
    exit, 109
    presentation, 107,109
    program, 109
    working, 107-109
*Preparing Tomorrow's Teachers to
    Use Technology. See* PT3
    grant
Prerequisite skills, 143-145
Presentation portfolios, 107,109
Principles of technology integration,
    15-23
    faculty design team approach,
        8-12,15-23
Problem-based learning, 25-42
    background and principles, 26-28
    conclusions, 38-40
    definition, 32
    design team activities, 31-38
    effectiveness study, 36-37
    forming design team, 28-31
    future plans, 38
    literacy methods course, 34-36
    science methods course, 33-34
    sharing findings, 37
Professional development, 56,115-125
    conclusions, 124-126
    data collection, 117-119
    faculty comments, 123-124
    mature experience in, 73-84
    results, 119-123
Professional growth, 5-6
Program portfolios, 109
PT3 program, 1-14
    definition, 26
    evaluation method, 7-8
    external evaluation, 181-183
    goals, objectives, and outcomes, 4-7

institution, 3-7
program, 2-3
Public-school collaboration, 7

Research, 52
Risk taking, 56

SITE Conference, 11,37,101,140
Situated evaluation, 7-8
Society for Information Technology
    Education. *See* SITE
Special education, 59-72
    academic outcomes, 63-64
    conclusions, 70-71
    course development, 65-69
    distance education and, 62-63
    handheld computers in, 65
    live courses, benefits of, 62
    personal development and, 65-66
    PT3 grant and, 64-65
    review of literature, 60-64
    student contributions, 69-70
    students' reception, 63

study/practice recommendations, 70
    WebQuests in, 67
Standards, 52
Students, electronic portfolio
        experiences, 111-112
Systemic change, 15-23

Teacher, image of, 48-49
Teamwork, 50
Tests, 52

Utah Education Network, 8

WebQuest design team, 20-22
WebQuests, 11
    definition, 33
    learning curve for, 35-36
    in problem-based learning, 30-31
    structured nature of, 36
    workshop in, 18
Working portfolios, 107-109

BOOK ORDER FORM!

Order a copy of this book with this form or online at:
http://www.haworthpress.com/store/product.asp?sku=5348

Integrating Information Technology
into the Teacher Education Curriculum
Process and Products of Change

_____ in softbound at $29.95 (ISBN: 0-7890-2628-7)
_____ in hardbound at $49.95 (ISBN: 0-7890-2627-9)

COST OF BOOKS _____

POSTAGE & HANDLING _____
US: $4.00 for first book & $1.50
for each additional book
Outside US: $5.00 for first book
& $2.00 for each additional book.

SUBTOTAL _____
In Canada: add 7% GST. _____

STATE TAX _____
CA, IL, IN, MN, NJ, NY, OH & SD residents
please add appropriate local sales tax.

FINAL TOTAL _____
If paying in Canadian funds, convert
using the current exchange rate.
UNESCO coupons welcome.

❏ BILL ME LATER:
Bill-me option is good on US/Canada/
Mexico orders only; not good to jobbers,
wholesalers, or subscription agencies.

❏ Signature _____

❏ Payment Enclosed: $ _____

❏ PLEASE CHARGE TO MY CREDIT CARD:
❏ Visa ❏ MasterCard ❏ AmEx ❏ Discover
❏ Diner's Club ❏ Eurocard ❏ JCB

Account # _____

Exp Date _____

Signature _____
(Prices in US dollars and subject to change without notice.)

PLEASE PRINT ALL INFORMATION OR ATTACH YOUR BUSINESS CARD

Name

Address

City   State/Province   Zip/Postal Code

Country

Tel   Fax

E-Mail

May we use your e-mail address for confirmations and other types of information? ❏ Yes ❏ No We appreciate receiving
your e-mail address. Haworth would like to e-mail special discount offers to you, as a preferred customer.
We will never share, rent, or exchange your e-mail address. We regard such actions as an invasion of your privacy.

Order From Your **Local Bookstore** or Directly From
The Haworth Press, Inc. 10 Alice Street, Binghamton, New York 13904-1580 • USA
Call Our toll-free number (1-800-429-6784) / Outside US/Canada: (607) 722-5857
Fax: 1-800-895-0582 / Outside US/Canada: (607) 771-0012
E-mail your order to us: orders@haworthpress.com

For orders outside US and Canada, you may wish to order through your local
sales representative, distributor, or bookseller.
For information, see http://haworthpress.com/distributors

(Discounts are available for individual orders in US and Canada only, not booksellers/distributors.)

Please photocopy this form for your personal use.
www.HaworthPress.com

BOF04